FROM THE LAND OF DIAMONDS TO THE ISLE OF SPICE

Sigismond Henry Tucker

Edited by
Winston Forde

From the Land of Diamonds to the Isle of Spice

Copyright © 2013 by Sigismund H Tucker

ISBN: 978-9988-1-8134-5

Printed in UK

Sierra Leonean Writers Series
c/o 42A Kofi Annan Ave., N-Legon, Accra, Ghana
c/o Mallam O. & J. Enterprises
120 Kissy Road, Freetown, Sierra Leone
www.sl-writers-series.org
writersseries.sl@gmail.com

This Book is dedicated

to

My mother Mrs Janet Lillian King, and our late son, Joe.

Front Cover Photograph

Author's note - From Left to right:
- *My late grandmother Fatoumata, died 10 years ago in Brazzaville*
- *The small child in hat is my mother Janet lives in Sierra Leone (now 87).
  She was taken to Freetown at the age of 14.*
- *My aunt Beatrice who is still in Brazzaville*

Acknowledgements

My special appreciation goes to my late friend, Ambrose Ganda, who inspired me to embark upon this book.

I would also like to thank my wife, Joan, my late son Joseph, and daughters Jasmine and Jean-Marie Tucker, who have put up with me during the ten years it has taken me to achieve this result.

My friend, Ade Daramy, who provided me with literary and technical support throughout.

Also, my friend Varsha Thakore, who typed the manuscripts

Finally, I am extremely grateful to my editor, Winston Forde, for sharing his outstanding skill as a seasoned author, together with his unrelenting zeal to help me fulfil my longstanding aspiration to publish this my first book.

Foreword

It is with great pleasure that I write to endorse this book 'From the land of Diamonds to the Isle of spice', a thoroughly clear-sighted, honest book that provides a personal, and political perspective by the author. The rendition on how he grew up in Sierra Leone, to his quest for further education in the United Kingdom, where he met his wife, Joan, from Grenada and had a family, to his discovery of his Congolese roots is impressive.

The book is captivating to me, partly because I have known the author through most of the times he has described, but I am particularly impressed with his narrative about the chronological events in Sierra Leone in the 1960s, and how they helped shape his life. His passion for Congolese music is unparalleled, before I knew he had any roots in the Congo, as we competed to memorize, and recite some melodies of the latest music coming from there without understanding a lick of what they were saying. His journey to England for further studies was no easy feat, and the need to balance work, and school to get by in order to reach his educational goals and subsequently to secure a series of jobs within the Civil Service proved challenging.

The most rewarding tribute is his commitment to his family, and the terrible experience of losing his son, Joe, with whom he had a special relationship; may his soul rest in perfect peace. I will not do this book any justice if I did not recognize the author's fixation for football, and his beloved Mighty Blackpool team of Sierra Leone where he mentioned most of the prominent footballers of our era. The book took me down memory lane with a dose of humor, and real people, endurance, and survival that the author narrated which helped to make him the successful man he is today.

Khelleh Konteh, BSBA, MA
Director, Ohio Prisons Industries.

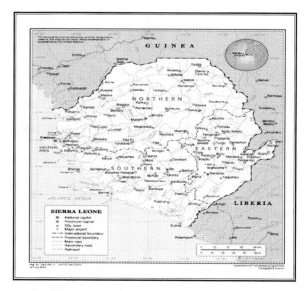

Maps of Sierra Leone and the Congo

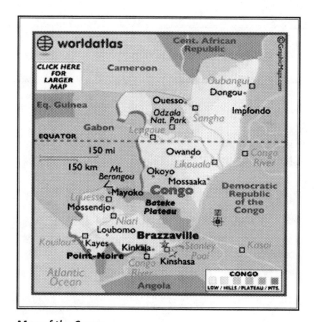

Map of the Congo

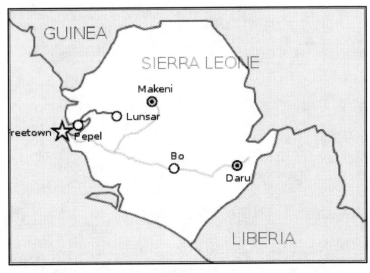

Maps of Sierra Leone and the Congo

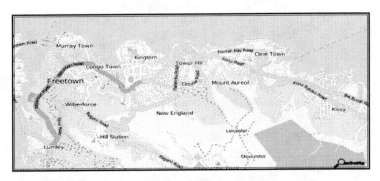

Map of the Congo

CONTENTS

Prologue

This is a true story, which encompasses two republics in Africa: Sierra Leone, in West Africa and Congo-Brazzaville in Central Africa.

Most of the characters in this story carry their true identity, but others have been given fictitious names to protect their identities.

This story began nineteen years before I was born as Sigismond Humble Tucker alias "Humble" on 1st October 1944.

Around 1925, three good friends left the port of Freetown, Sierra Leone, on a merchant ship. The first, Christopher Williams, later became my grandfather, I.T.A Wallace Johnson, who later became a well known if controversial journalist, trade unionist, and politician both in Ghana in the 1950s and Sierra Leone in the late 60s until his death. The third friend was the less well known, Mr Thompson.

The merchant ship arrived in Matadi, a famous port in the Congo. It stayed in port for about a week, discharging merchandise and uploading fresh cargo. Even in those days, sailors would go into the main town seeking excitement, amusement and entertainment.

Accordingly, the three friends went into town for a drink and ended up in a bar owned by an American businessman who had lived in the Congo for some time, and had established businesses all over Brazzaville.

They impressed him with their fluency in English, and more especially Christopher, so he enquired of them

"Where do you three come from, and what brought you to Brazzaville?"

"We are seamen," Christopher answered, "and we shall be going back to Freetown in a week's time."

"How much salary do you earn working on that ship?"

They earned less than the American could offer them. He explained that he came from America, and had amassed huge wealth doing business in Brazzaville. He proposed to these three men that they should consider working for him; he liked Christopher especially, and wanted to pass on some of his business responsibilities as manager of most of his stores.

After some negotiations, they agreed terms, and the three men never returned to their ship. They remained in Brazzaville long after she had sailed. Christopher moved to an interior district called Quesso, with a very rich town - much like Kono district in Sierra Leone with Yengema where most diamonds are mined. Diamonds remain one of the main sources of income in these two countries. However, Kono District in Sierra Leone had always been full of foreigners from all parts of the world, especially the Lebanese in great numbers. Originally, they would come to do small business in Freetown, but intending to move to the diamond mining areas. Whereas the Congolese government only allowed indigenous Congolese to settle in Quesso. This major difference has caused serious problems in Sierra Leone for decades, as I shall reveal later in the book.

Having stayed on, Christopher became well established, and quickly became an efficient business manager. Naturally, he soon decided to get a girlfriend, and started an early relationship with a beautiful Gabonese lady, by the name of Caroline Tikalé. They went out for a few months until he came across a very beautiful local lady by the name of Fatoumata, originally from Senegal. Their romance developed, and eventually they got married. They were blessed with two daughters named Janet Lillian and Beatrice. The former subsequently became my mother.

Christopher had a sister who lived in Hastings, Kossoh Town on the outskirts of Freetown called Lillian Cole alias "Mamma Lillie". She had an only son by the name of Joko Cole also of Kossoh Town who worked for a shipping company in Cline Town in Freetown.

After many years in Brazzaville owning several businesses, and having amassed considerable wealth, the American decided to end his sojourn in Africa to go back to America. Behaving somewhat strangely, he unexpectedly called Christopher and said, "I've had enough, you have been an invaluable business colleague all these years. I feel that it was time to return to America, and I want you to have the rest of the businesses". Christopher couldn't believe what he heard; it was like a dream.

Thus, Christopher became the owner of this vast business empire with his wife Fatoumata and their two daughters, Janet Lillian and Beatrice. Already a wealthy man, he had quite a number of people working for him. Servants carried him everywhere in a hammock like a Chief, as a practical symbol of his wealth. During one of these outings his entourage came across a buffalo that had been shot. Unbeknown to them, the beast had only been injured, but not killed. Christopher asked his men to put him down, so he could take a closer look. Sadly, the buffalo then attacked him so ferociously on his chest, causing some serious injuries from which he never fully recovered until his death a few years later.

By this time the two girls were growing up nicely in the Congo. Christopher contemplated sending them to Kossoh Town in Hastings near Freetown to be cared for by his sister before his death. But, when he suggested this idea to Fatoumata, she would not yield to him saying, "Over my dead body" as their tribal custom did not allow for children to be separated from their family.

With his very good persuasive skills, though, they agreed a compromise, and agreed that Lillian should be taken to Kossoh Town to live with her aunt. Beatrice remained in the Congo with Fatoumata at Quesso until she got married and moved to Pointe Noire. Fortuitously, Mr Thompson had planned to travel to Freetown, and he undertook to escort Lillian to Kossoh Town. She was a 12 -year -old girl who spoke only Lingala and Bakongo. She took along her birth certificate, Congolese passport, traditional clothes, and lots of money to help Mama Lillie with the cost of her upkeep. Her sick father, Christopher, died a year afterwards and her Congolese family did not see Lillian again until 1988 at a much delayed family reunion! One can imagine what this little girl felt on her arrival in Freetown, a strange land and where they spoke a strange language. Everybody called her 'Congo girl'.

I have sometimes wondered why we have areas in and around Freetown, with names like Congo Town, Congo Cross, Congo Market and often ask myself whether these towns were named as a result of Sierra Leoneans from the Congo coming back to settle in those areas, or Congolese coming to Sierra Leone to settle. However, as we never hear any authentic Congolese names in these areas, I am forced to conclude they date much further back to the 19th century when Americo-Liberians immigrated to become founders of Liberia and other colonies along the coast in places that would become Cote d'Ivoire and Sierra Leone. Later, these African Americans integrated 5,000 liberated Africans called Congos (descendants of former slaves from the Congo Basins who never made it to the Americas) and 346 Barbadian immigrants into the hegemony.

Mr I.T.A. Wallace-Johnson stayed in the Congo for a few years and had some children who had Congolese names, according to tradition. Luckily for me our Congolese family carried both the Christopher Williams Tamod and the Congolese names, which assisted me greatly in tracing them later. For example a cousin of mine is called Christopher Tamod Williams. Mr Thompson went back to the Congo and settled down, had children again carrying Congolese names. One of his sons is now Professor of Economics and Development at the University of Brazzaville. On a recent visit to Brazzaville

I met them when they came to introduce themselves as having origins from Sierra Leone.

A son of a poor Creole family born in 1894, Wallace-Johnson became a British West African workers' leader, journalist, activist and politician after emerging as a natural leader in school. After attending the United Methodist Collegiate School, for just two years, he dropped out to take a job as an officer in the customs department in 1913. He lost this job in 1926, and left Sierra Leone to become a sailor, a decision that would take him to the Congo on that fateful voyage with Christopher. He joined a national seamen's union, and it is believed that he also joined the Communist Party, in 1930.

Within a few months of returning to Nigeria in1933, the authorities deported him because of his illicit trade union activities. He travelled to the Gold Coast, where he quickly established himself as a political activist and journalist. In 1935, Wallace-Johnson met Nnamdi Azikwe, the future nationalist President of Nigeria, in Accra. Azikiwe tried to dissociate himself from Wallace-Johnson's Marxist ideologies, as he believed his own ideas were not remotely compatible with those of his fellow politician. Both men believed that a renaissance needed to occur in Africa, but they disagreed over the methods of doing so. Each man believed that his own idea would prevail in the future. Azikiwe described his first meeting with Wallace-Johnson as such:

"We exchanged views and I said that while I thought that it would be practicable for Africans at this stage of development to experience an intellectual revolution, yet an extremist or leftist point of view would be dangerous, in view of the unpreparedness of the masses. He countered by pointing out the fate of Soviet Russia, where the masses were illiterate and impoverished, and yet when Lenin, Stalin, and Trotsky sounded the clarion, they rallied round them and a new order emerged. I warned him that his analogy was false, because Russia was unlike West Africa; the political, social and economic situations were different. He told me point blank that if Africans depended upon intellectuals or leaders of thought, they would not get beyond the stage of producing orators and resolution-passers. It was necessary for doers or leaders of action to step on the scene and prove that the African has a revolutionary spirit in him." — Nnamdi Azikiwe, *My Odyssey: An Autobiography (1970)*. .

After meeting Nnamdi Azikwe in 1935, Wallace-Johnson formed the West African Youth League (WAYL), an organization dedicated to obtaining more liberties and privileges for the Gold Coast population. Wallace-Johnson and the WAYL entered the Gold Coast political scene by supporting Kojo Thompson in his successful candidacy in the Legislative Council elections of 1935.

He returned to Sierra Leone in 1938 and established a number of labor unions, a newspaper and a political movement. He remained a troublesome activist until his arrest on 1 September 1939 under the Emergency Act adopted at the start of World War 2 earlier that day. Wallace-Johnson was put on trial without a jury, and received a 12-month prison sentence, which he served on Sherbro Island before his release in1944. He returned to political activism, but found the WAYL in a state of disarray. He merged the league into the National Council of Sierra Leone, but left for Ghana just before their independence gained on 6th March 1957. He studied journalism, politics, and worked in Ghana for several years embracing Pan Africanism under President Kwame Nkruma with whom he had a very good political relationship. He enjoyed much love and affection in Ghana and had family there too. He had a son in Sierra Leone called E.B. Wallace-Johnson, a well known National Football Association referee; he also took part in Sierra Leone Athletics , and was later appointed Director of National Sports.

After many years in Ghana, Mr I.T.A. Wallace Johnson finally returned to Sierra Leone, and settled down at Wilberforce Village. He opened his own small press and edited his own newspaper. Added to that, he actively engaged in politics as a founding member of the United Progressive Party (U.P.P). He served as a delegate from Sierra Leone during independence talks in London in 1960. Also, as a member of the Board of Governors of the West African Methodist Collegiate School, our alma mater, he provided regular support and advice to the principal, Mr J.A. Garber. The Freetown based U.P.P's main campaigning idea claimed that Freetown belonged to the settlers freed from slavery who had returned home and settled in Freetown. A party with such ideas could not penetrate outside Freetown, and therefore could only win seats in Freetown lCity Council elections. Around that period, people like Bankole Bright, Columbus Thompson, J.A Galba-Bright,

Alderman E.R.G Davies and many more from 'settler families' became councillors in Freetown.

Isaac Theophilus Akunna Wallace-Johnson

Sadly, in May of 1965, I.T.A. Wallace Johnson died in a road accident in Ghana. The Sierra Leone government declared a period of national mourning. When Dr Kwame Nkrumah heard of his death he sent a beautiful gold-plated casket as a gift in recognition of his service to Ghana. At the state funeral held in his beloved Wilberforce Village, the undertakers draped his casket with the National Flag, and the Flag of the Collegiate School.

Chapter 1

My Childhood

My father, Joseph Tucker, hailed from Bonthe Sherbro Island in the Southern Province of Sierra Leone. He later moved to Hastings, a village east of Kissy, where he had some Mende relatives, and served his apprenticeship in carpentry under his uncle, Tommy Charlice, a well-known carpenter.

My mother, Janet Lillian, lived with her guardian Mama Lilly Cole, the sister of my grandfather, Christopher Williams. Mama Lilly Cole had one son by the name of Joko Cole of Carr Street, Kossoh Town, Hastings. He grew up with my mother, and they were like brother and sister. Many regarded my mother, fresh, bright and beautiful originating from Congo-Brazzaville, as one of the main beauty sensations in town! She caught the eye of a teacher at the Hastings Primary School, which she attended, named Mr. B A King. Wholly inappropriately, even in those days, a boyfriend/girlfriend relationship developed, and they eventually produced a child, Beatrice Koryeh. Mr. King later moved to Freetown taking custody of Koryeh, and later married another lady. He became a popular schoolteacher in Freetown, especially at the West African Methodist Collegiate Secondary School where he eventually became Vice-principal. He went on to lecture at the Milton Margai Teacher Training College at Goderich Village, and eventually became the Principal of Freetown Teachers College at Fourah Bay Road.

After Mr. B.A King left Hastings for Freetown to continue his teaching career, my mother had a new

1

suitor named Joseph Tucker. She described him to me as being handsome, tall and kind, "just like you". The relationship got deeper, and soon she fell pregnant. She told me once that she suffered from morning sickness throughout the pregnancy. Apparently, I was always kicking her, and maybe that's where I started my lasting obsession with football. "Eventually, I gave birth to you, quietly without any complications," she told me later. My parents christened me Sigismond Henry Abioseh Humble Tucker, but neighbours and friends of the family called me "Sherbro boy." I grew up with my mother, and father in Hastings until aged four years. My father's relative, a Mende woman called Mama Boiye took care of me most of the time.

We moved to Fort Street in Freetown and my father got a job as a carpenter in a saw mill along Soldier Street, near a place called "Samba Gutter" by a huge open drain, one of several that swelled up with red muddy lateritic water during the rainy season, and flowed from the hills and mountains down into the river forming a red pattern in the sea at the mouth of the bays, and harbour. They found him a very good tradesman, and rapidly made him a supervisor. Joseph soon became very popular in the Mende community in that area of Freetown. In fact, he became one of the leaders of the local Gorboiye Society, a Mende cultural society in Sierra Leone. I remember as a young boy, when the Gorboiye Society were performing for the day, my dad would get rid of us children from the house for the day, to enable them to perform all their ceremonies in secret. Apart from his cultural involvement with this tribal society, he also loved football. Maybe that made me develop my intense love for the game, as well.

Our house in Fort Street stood about 15 minutes walk from Tower Hill, a military garrison area, and the nearby Army Parade Square served as a local football ground aptly known as "Parade Ground". My father took me there regularly to watch the Army team known as the 'Frontier Rangers' play.

The West African Frontier Force (WAFF) was formed by the British Colonial Office in 1900 to administer the regular colonial forces of West Africa. They raised the majority of the WAFF in Nigeria, their base, but there were also units located in The Gold Coast (now Ghana), Sierra Leone and The Gambia. The units were:

The Queen's Own Nigeria Regiment
The Gold Coast Regiment
The Royal Sierra Leone Regiment
The Gambia Regiment

In 1928 WAFF gained the title of the Royal West African Frontier Force (RWAFF) and in 1940 reorganised as infantry; support elements being transferred to African Colonial Forces (with suffix "A.C.F." to unit titles). The RWAFF served in the 81st and 82nd West African Divisions, 14th Army against the Japanese in Burma. Units from the Gambia, Nigeria, Sierra Leone and the Gold Coast formed the 81st, while the 82nd comprised units from Nigeria and the Gold Coast. In 1946 the RWAFF further reorganised as infantry combined with internal support elements. In 1953 Gold Coast Military Forces were established as the first national force within RWAFF and in 1959 Ghana (former Gold Coast) withdrew from RWAFF. In 1960 WAFF disbanded after all the units were absorbed into Royal

Nigerian Military Forces, Royal Sierra Leone Military Forces, and Ghana Army. I still recall those early British officers in their distinctive khaki uniforms and shorts with a long strip of brown cloth wound spirally around their legs from ankle to knee for protection and support known as puttees, and wearing black army boots. Many years were to pass before local soldiers were promoted as officers some of whom invariably became entangled in our national politics with some dreadful consequences.

My mother, Janet, remained a strong practising Christian, and brought us up with good Christian values. When we moved to Fort Street, she and I attended 'Zion on the Hill' church. Most times I accompanied her to help clean the church on Saturdays in preparation for service on Sundays. This would have been about 1948-49, until my father secured low-cost housing accommodation at Syke Street in Ascension Town. They called them "Pilot Houses" and we were amongst the first tenants to move to that estate. These were affordable bungalows with one and two bedrooms. There were also two-storey buildings for the high earners. I remember one of the popular tenants in those days, a famous police inspector, commonly known as "mago-mago Wright" because he always reported first at the scene of a crime. We struck up a close family relationship with one of our new neighbours, the Jamirus. Mr Jamiru worked as a medical dispenser at the Connaught Hospital, and he and his younger brother Kapindi Jamiru lived in the two-bedroom bungalow next door to ours.

Connaught Hospital served as the main civilian hospital in Freetown, and is located centrally, but along the coast at the bottom of Percival Street abutting Water Street(now

Wallace-Johnson Street). It is also the main referral hospital in Sierra Leone. Initially opened in1912 by the Duke of Connaught, President Kabbah re-opened it in May 2006. During our colonial days this hospital provided quite good medical service for our people. At present it has very basic equipment and although the building has been recently redecorated it is still very under equipped. However, care at the hospital is improving and in 2009 doctors reported a fall in complications and deaths in the maternity ward.

I felt like a little brother to Kapindi who took me everywhere he went. At that time I admired him as a very clever senior boy at the Methodist Boys High School, and an excellent footballer. He often played for Richmond, the division one team of the School at the Association Grounds in King Tom, where all division one games were played, as a very popular footballer playing alongside well known players like Boye Davies of Richmond and Kester Campbell. At home my father resumed his cultural activities with the Gorboiye society, and they held dances in the extensive grounds of the Syke Street pilot houses, which attracted people in the area.

In 1950, my mother got a job as sales assistant in a shop owned by the late Mr. Emmanuel R.G Davies, a well-known businessman in Freetown, and an Alderman of the City Council. He had three children - the famous Dr. Marcela Davies and her brothers Roland and Harry Davies. My mother worked for a while in the shop at Wellington Street, and being impressed with her performance, Pa Davies, asked her to manage another shop at Congo Town in 1951. Sadly, as a result, we had to move from Syke Street. By this time my friend Kapindi's elder brother had moved to Pendembu to practice dispensary leaving him on his own. So, we invited Kapindi to come and stay with us, as the shop at Congo Town had three bedrooms at the back, pending his entry to Fourah Bay College on Mount Aureol, which for decades was affiliated with Durham University. We were sad to see him go, but he would always come down to visit us whenever students came down on holidays. He went on to graduate with a B.A degree, and then later became Assistant Secretary, Permanent Secretary and Provincial Secretary. Eventually he left government service and contested elections and ended up as a government minister. What a fabulous career befitting one so clever! He maintained his links with our family long after I left for England, and regularly visited, and took care of my mother until his death a few years ago. I cried when I got the news here in England, and more especially from my inability to attend the funeral, that precious final rite held in such reverence by our people.

Around 1951-52 my father, Joseph, started to make frequent visits to Bo and Kenema, but I did not know whether he went on business or had another woman in one of these towns, and the matter was never discussed with me as a young boy of about seven years. On one of those trips, he left and never came back. Word reached my mother after many enquiries suggesting he now lived in Kenema, working in the Forest Industry Corporation. I had no idea whether to believe this or not, but thought it a feasible outcome for a very good carpenter. However, this taught me another salutary lesson about the nature of adult relationships amongst the Creoles of Freetown. On the one hand, as practising Christians they strove to maintain rather strict Victorian standards and values, yet they practised a pervading culture of promiscuity, and freedom in sexual relationships. Single people would meet, indulge, and produce a child who may or may not receive full attention from both parents, and even married men would sometimes produce children with married women who would never own up. As the general edict stated that a married woman could not have a bastard child, no child could openly be acknowledged as having been born to parents out of wedlock; but no one questioned just how much of that existed in our society. From this point onwards life became a struggle for my mother was forced to bring up my brother,Tunde Edward Woode, and myself single-handedly, but somehow she managed to do so. She received reasonable earnings at the shop at Congo Town, and our free accommodation helped greatly. We were both enrolled at the primary section of Roosevelt Secondary School, founded in 1952 by a remarkable woman, Mrs. Constance Cummings-John.

Born in 1918 into a prominent Creole family much involved in community affairs and local business, it may have been inevitable that she should be interested in politics. The young Constance received her early education in Freetown: Annie Walsh Memorial School, Methodist Girls' High School and Freetown Secondary School for Girls. She proceeded to England to train as a teacher. In London, she also found time to participate in the activities of two Pan-African Organisations, the West African Students' Union (WASU) and the League of Coloured Peoples (LCP). Both were pressure groups fighting the African cause. In 1936 she went to the United States to do a six-month course at Cornell

University. It was a shocking experience. The racial insults heaped on her, and the lack of understanding from Afro-Americans affected her political consciousness profoundly. Depressed but undaunted, she resolved to return home and "throw the white man out." In 1937, she married Ethanan Cummings-John, a lawyer, and the same year saw them return to Sierra Leone.

On being appointed Principal of the A.M.E. Girls' Vocational School, popularly known as the Roosevelt School, she found the school in a dilapidated state, and immediately embarked on a fund-raising campaign to make improvements. Through this venture, she pioneered the construction of a new domestic science building with modern equipment. The school flourished under her leadership, and became well known in Freetown as a vocational institute. Also, in recognition of the importance of women in community affairs, she established a network of leading market women; in 1951, with their support, she established the Sierra Leone Women's Movement, which played a leading role in the struggle for self-government. After independence, Mrs. Constance Cummings-John became the first woman mayor of the Freetown Municipality.

In 1953, Edward and I transferred to Murray Town Primary School.

From that time on, I never saw my father, Joseph, again. In 1968 when I was working in the Law Courts in Freetown, news came that he had died in Kenema. Whether this was true or not made no difference to me; he had been gone for years out of my life, so why should I care?

My mother continued to nurture me, and took full responsibility for my development. My personal experience as a one-parent child made me vow that I would look after my own children, and not abandon them. I am proud to say that I have looked after my wife and three children, who are all university graduates, including Joe who tragically passed away in 2009. Joan, and I are in our 36th year of marriage, and we have never turned our backs on our children. Sadly, the immoral practices, and worrying sexual standards have persisted in our country to this day, and there's still much work to be done in that respect.

Alderman Mrs Constance Cummings-John

=========== **Chapter 2** ===========

Growing up with Doctor Major-General Momoh

What can I say of Joseph Saidu Momoh, the man who would later succeed Siaka Stevens as President? His rapid rise to power, I saw coming when he was a key witness in the trial of Brigadier Juxon-Smith for treason. At that time ,in 1969, myself and Alex Kamara acted as clerks of court, with Chief Justice C.O.E. Cole as the trial judge.

I remember Joseph, then an Army captain, taking the oath at the witness stand, holding the Bible in one hand: "I Joseph Saidu Momoh, hereby promise to tell the truth, the whole truth, and nothing but the truth, so help me God". At the end of that trial, when Juxon-Smith was given a life sentence for treason, the rapid rise of Saidu Joseph began in earnest. He was promoted to Major. Within the space of another two years when Siaka Stevens was President, he became Major-General, and finally Brigadier, by which time he had become a politician in the making.

At that time, I enjoyed a strong friendship with Momoh, in fact we had known each other from the late 50s when he was attending Collegiate School. At the time, the school was located at Circular Road, and my mother, Sissy, managed the shop.

Our usual meeting place at the top of Congo Cross was an area called "Four-Road" (a four way intersection) long before Juxon-Smith built the present fountain. "Four-Road" was a market place, where CongoTown Market stood years before.

Also there was Jehovah Shammah Church, which was my Church, opposite the Tweede family home. The Tweedes were a prominent business family in Congo Town. They had the bakery which supplied bread to the whole town.

My relationship as a friend of the Momoh family went back to those days; they used to live in a house constructed from corrugated iron at the back of Methodist Girls High School.

Traders from Wilberforce, Murray Town, Lumley, and Goderich would all meet at "Four-Road". This place was the next big market place after Kroo Town Road market, King Jimmy, Kissy Road and Dove Court markets. I would meet friends such as the Momoh brothers, Pa Koroma ,who had the palm wine bar, his sons Santigi Koroma and Sinneh Koroma, their cousin, Dinneh Koroma, to gossip at night time about the latest news in town, talk about women, and school.

Similarly, the Samba brothers, Jallah, Boye, who were my good friends, would join me at the Four-Road after playing football. An old lady called Grandma Dalmas, owned vast acres of land at Wilberforce, including an old tennis court where we used to play tennis in the evenings, for money. We called it "bite game" (literally a betting game), and stakes were sometimes one or two shillings, winners take all! In those days Sierra Leone's currency comprised pounds, shillings and pence, having the same value as the British currency.

At this time, around the late fifties, Joseph Saidu Momoh was attending the West African Methodist Collegiate School at Circular Road. He would come to the shop in the mornings before going to school, dropping his empty kerosene container, and collecting it full of kerosene after school. I can still picture him, hanging his jacket over his shoulder. In those days Collegiate pupils had to wear jackets as part of the school juniform, and others used to call us "chinch coat" (chinch being bed bugs).

His older brother worked for the Wilberforce District Council, not too far from where they lived. He was in the sanitation department, cutting grass and hedges around the roads. He was the least educated, but his other brothers all attended Collegiate school. By this time the new building was located at Wilkinson Road. William Momoh was in same class as me and the one before William, Parloh Momoh was in the 4th form. He too joined the army after leaving school. By that time J. S. Momoh was already a Captain in the army, and had already started his rapid rise. Parloh Momoh was commissioned as a First Lieutenant, and by the time I visited Sierra Leone, a few years later in December 1990, he was a Major.

When Joseph Saidu Momoh and his friend Patrick Foyah were commissioned as Lieutenants they visited Collegiate school regularly in their smart uniforms. To me this was not simply to show-off, but I felt these were motivational visits that inspired us to take our education seriously so that we too would become good citizens. This is relevant to my story because, here I was, looking up to someone whom I felt was a very useful citizen and very professional, who inspired me to develop my education.

During this time I was in the first form, which was in the 1961-62 school year. Little did we know that Momoh, an Old Boy of the school, would turn out to become president of Sierra Leone. Some hold the view that being a military man, he should have adopted a firm grip on the evils of society, and not allow the country to further deteriorate as a victim of politics.

—————————— **Chapter 3** ——————————

My formative years

Freetown, capital of Sierra Leone, nestles on the northern side of a peninsula with the estuary of the Rokel River forming its northern seaboard, and natural harbour. A chain of mountains forms a solid core to the peninsula, serving as a picturesque and sheltering background. It served as the railhead of the tiny 18-inch gauge railway that snaked its way for 136 miles across wide river valleys, and through thick tropical vegetation to the inland Town of Bo. Freetown had been settled by freed slaves, and out of these the Creoles had developed into a core of intelligentsia amongst the indigenous people. They adopted western names like Jones and Smith, and a western style of dress, and were in all the administrative, and official positions in the Church, and colonial administration in which local people were allowed to be employed.

Moving away from the city where the people lived in homes which were of mixed architectural design, and on to the surrounding hills, most of the colonial servants lived in more pleasant surroundings at Hill Station and Wilberforce, each with his own domestic staff. Several coastal villages bearing English names such as Aberdeen, Kent, York, and Goderich are found on the western side of the peninsula, and on the east we had Cline Town, Kissy, Wellington, and Hastings.

I spent most of my boyhood, and teenage years in the western sector of Freetown. My mother married Bankole King, namesake of her earlier suitor, and a sea-farer from Murray Town in 1958. We left Congo Town in1959 to move to our new home, and this wrench caused me to cry as we were leaving. I remembered how I used to attend Jehovah Shamah Methodist Church, opposite the Tweed and Roberts family homes. The old postmaster, known as Pa Thompson lived further up, not far from the church. I used to go and help him and his wife domestically because they were a very nice elderly couple who had no children living with them. The family move pleased me, though, as I found Murray Town to be a lovely village, with a beautiful coastline, and a close community, most of whom were connected with the fishing industry. Indeed, the village Headman, Pa Sonny John, later handed over to Mr. Bright, the father of the well-known S.L.B.S broadcaster, Mr. Sylvanus Bright. We had our own village police station right at the bottom of Highbroad Street, near the community centre. Two main churches served the Christian community, including Ebenezer Methodist Church on Highbroad Street just by the school compound. Part of the school operated from Macaulay Street, in the same compound as a West African Methodist church known as Jordan Church. We lived in a house on Milton Street, owned by my stepfather, Mr. Bankole King, which he inherited from his grandmother, Granny Drucilla King. It loomed large as a very big two story wooden house of the style introduced by the settlers, and we had tenants in the cellar, some very popular fellows in the village, most of whom were fishermen. Men like Bansha, also Fonti Kamara who took very much to me; he used to call me "Backstore". He would go fishing for 2-3 weeks and would catch and keep fish especially for me. He called this special supply "Backstores" and I soon inherited that nick name from him. Murray Town boasted one of the first modern fishing industries in the country dating from the early fifties, and for many years Italians, who seemed to be all over the village, controlled everything. I can recall two popular trawlers, "Hombrina" and "Batista". Some of the Italians married local women and had children in Murray Town and surrounding areas, including Cole Farm and Aberdeen Road areas. However, when some of these latino men left, the children or their mothers never heard from them afterwards.

Although I did not fully realise it then, Freetown had its heyday experiencing the best levels that commerce and industry would be at for years to come. Central Freetown lay about five miles away with a whole range of administrative and managerial jobs in the health services and other government departments. In addition, Murray Town had a booming Fishing Industry. Local people had jobs, working in the docks by the bay, fishing or transporting fish. They called it "White Man's" Bay. Fishermen took to the sea in trawlers for weeks at a time. There were limited provisions for marine engineering, and the docks were busy repairing boats, so there were ample technical jobs for our people as well in the area. My mother continued to manage Mr. Davies's shop, and through her hard work that shop and bar became the most popular in the vicinity. She sold all types of beers, cigarettes, lager and alcohol, and after a hard day's work, the Italians would gravitate to our shop to enjoy themselves. We sold popular brands of wine such as Cock Vermouth, which reminds me of an old, well-liked, customer called Pa Ansumana. He had very few teeth in his mouth. He liked drinking Cock Vermouth, and whenever he came to the shop we knew exactly what he wanted, but he had a funny way of pronouncing the name of the wine. He would call out to my mum, "Janet, Janet, give me one cock Barmbot". We used to crack up in fits of laughter at this, because the word "Barmbot" in the local slang referred to a prostitute. Other brands of wine that were popular with the locals included Santa Maria, and Kini-Kini.

Soon, we had a few Italian friends especially one called Michele, the captain of the trawler "Hombrina". He would let us know his arrival times so that we could go and meet them to be given free fish. Sometimes he would give us two to three boxes of fish, assorted shrimps, lobsters and "conk" (sea snail). A lot of the times we had so much fish that I took some for my stepsister, Beatrice, who lived with her father and stepmother.

We had another small house in our yard, occupied by Pa Freeman. He too worked as a fisherman, and also acted as one of the "Agba's" of the village 'ogun-gun society'. "Agba" means leader. We also had Papa Dosumu further up Milton Street, another fisherman of high status in the society. I further knew him as one of the elders of Ebenezer Church which I attended, and where I received my confirmation, together with my brother Edward. Pa Arthur Lewis lived next door, and owned the village "Hunting Society". Santigie, who owned the village "Jorlay" society or "Alikali", lived as a tenant in our house. We enjoyed much African and traditional culture in the town, and these various people had much influence on my cultural upbringing, and discipline as a young boy growing up. In those days, we didn't have a mosque in Murray Town, so our muslim villagers would go for prayers at a mosque at Congo Cross, privately owned by an Imam called Pa Cole or "Maslasi" Cole, a local word for mosque.

Much of my life revolved around my schooling. We had teachers like Mr. E.T.O Alhakor, M.O.J.T Sackey, Miss Aina

Williams and Mrs. Manley, the latter two from Wilberforce. Our head teacher, Mr. J (John) Williams later handed over to Mr. J.O.O Williams. Mr. John Williams and Mr. Norman, the Sports master were the ones who liked to cane us pupils. To us, it seemed that when those men had their domestic problems at home, they would come to school and take it out on the children by flogging them for the slightest misdemeanour. John Williams, the headmaster had a nickname, "Momoh Loko". When he took the physical education class, and if one made a mistake during drill, he would cane you until his eyes were as red as if he had just finished smoking two or three joints of "diamba", the local name for marijuana or cannabis. Physical punishment became rampant in our day, which took the saying 'spare the rod and spoil the child' to the utmost. It should have been designated as child abuse!

Once in a while the government Public Relations Officer would go around the villages to show British newsreels on a mobile screen. We always looked forward to that form of enjoyment. Murray Town had an edge over surrounding villages in that it had the military headquarters, where they showed good war and cowboy films from England and America every Wednesday. They charged an entrance fee of one shilling, so if you could afford it, you were able to attend the shows starting at 8.00 p.m. to finish by 9.30 p.m. One evening, at the village school playgrounds, the bigger boys in the village plotted to give "Momoh Loko" a taste of his own medicine. They singled him out after the show and gave him a good beating. He wanted to run away, but they prevented him from all sides and he had nowhere to hide. Eventually, somebody managed to take him away in his car. We saw the event, and felt sorry for him, yet the rest of the pupils were very pleased. He did not come back to school for a few weeks.

About a year later, Mr. J.O.O Williams, who proved a complete opposite in terms of his dealings with pupils, succeeded "Momoh Loko".

A place called "Oloshoro," on the coastal area below the Murray Town Barracks Depot, became a popular spot from where people could get natural spring water. Oloshoro stream had been in existence long before Guma Valley Dam provided Freetown with tap water, and traditionally most inhabitants of Murray Town and nearby Cole Farm fetched water from this place. All kinds of spooky stories were associated with Oloshoro, so most people would go there in groups, and others were scared of going there in the dark. A popular myth claimed that an uncircumcised boy should not venture down there, as "the devil" would circumcise him. That tendency in our society to harbour tales of myth and intrigue played a significant part in our lives as children. It was always crowded, and people often made more than one trip. Young boys and girls would sometimes play pranks, and some would be caned for going home late with their buckets full of water. There were a few other water wells dug across the village, and the one closest to where we lived was on the opposite end of Milton Street, approaching the coastline.

We regarded Oloshoro water as a precious commodity; it was mostly for drinking. It reminds me of a town in England called Buxton in Cheshire, also famous for its natural spring water. An English friend of mine called Steve Bentley who lives in Buxton once invited me and my family to go and

spend the day with him. He took us around, and we saw natural springs all over the place, with water oozing from the ground. Hence today, we have Buxton mineral water, bottled and sold all over the United Kingdom. I am forced to muse that in a more organised situation, the same could be done with the water at Oloshoro, and I have little doubt such bottled water would be of extremely high quality.........
another of our lost opportunities in my country.

Soon the Italians, who managed the fisheries company, departed. The Koreans succeeded them for a few years, before the whole industry transferred to Kissy Dock Yard with devastating effects on employment prospects in our beloved Murray Town. We felt sad when we had to leave 16 Milton Street for the other end of Murray Town in 1961 to help look after the great Pastor Emmanuel Edwards, who had trained as a pastor in Philadelphia in the 40s and 50s. He had returned to Freetown from America with a burning ambition to build his own church, so he bought a vast piece of land in Byrne Lane, covered all over with bushes and fruit trees. Amongst the first inhabitants in that area were the Lewis Family, descendants of the famous Sir Samuel Lewis, Mama Dina Brown, the Kolleh family of "big yard", Mama Gordon, Pa Cole (Grammar School bursar) with a massive piece of land at the junction owned by a member of the Browne-Marke family.

Further down Aberdeen Ferry Road, going towards the Old Jetty, where they first attempted to build the Aberdeen Bridge, lived Pa Mansaray and his sons, Musa and Sheku. Their house stood just as one approached the famous landmark, and popular underground spring called Odoke. Everybody went to fetch drinking water from Odoke, just like "Oloshoro" at Murray Town. This is just a brief scenario of Aberdeen Ferry Road and Byrne Lane with its bush and marshland in the days when illicit Omole cooking was rife. Anyone caught cooking Omole (local gin) otherwise known as "Apatashe" would be arrested. Pa Foday partly owned what is now Thompson Bay at the back of Collegiate School, and the thick bush provided ample cover for the illegal Omole operations that the police found difficult to patrol.

All this became my new environment when we went to live with Pastor Edwards and his wife Mama Aina. They had plenty of food, so my younger brother, Tunde, and I never went hungry. Before Pastor Edwards started building his church, Hephzibah, we held services under a mango tree nearby, and when it rained we held services in the house. We had lots of members because people felt unable to travel to churches in Murray Town or Congo Town. Pastor Edwards used to say, "Where two or three are gathered in my name, I'm in the midst of them". He turned his extensive portion of land with big boulders of stone into a quarry hiring two good workers, "Sorie Katti" and "Sabi-Sabi" to produce stones for house building. During the building of his massive house at Wilkinson Road, Pa George Panda, the first secretary to Sir Milton Margai, got supplies of stones and boulders from us, and so did many other people. Pastor used the proceeds from the sale of these stones and boulders to start the Hephzibah church project. He used the fertile land to grow vegetables, and of course lots of fruits like mangoes, oranges, grapefruit, guava, papaya, and plums. My brother and I knew the bush inside out. We picked mangoes and other fruits -bags of them, and on Saturdays we would sell our harvest at Kissy Road Market using the bus services from Oxford Street (now Lightfoot-

Boston Street) to Aberdeen Ferry Road. We considered it a blessing going to live with Pastor Edwards. Looking at his quarry, he used to shake his head and say, "We Africans are walking on top of gold and yet we are so poor."

As time went on, he started to sell parts of the land, to raise money to build the church, but did not live long enough to complete it. Gradually, in the late sixties people started moving into Byrne Lane and building houses. His health started to deteriorate. On the eve of Independence, April 26th, 1961, he passed away after a short illness. He shared the often expressed belief that we were not yet ready for independence, and during his lifetime he prayed that he did not want to see an Independent Sierra Leone. His passing at that time, therefore, proved to be timely if not an interesting coincidence! We did not enjoy our Independence celebrations because of the passing of our dear guardian. He left a partly completed church with a wish that it should be handed over to the Methodist Church in Murray Town.

MT Rovers – Murray Town's village football team (me holding the ball)

———————————— **Chapter 4** ————————————

Our good old days

When I consider the present state of my beautiful country it makes me wonder, and I am tempted to ask the question, why? As I grew up, Sierra Leone seemed promising, and mainly trouble free, possibly apart from the Second World War when the British recruited some 375,000 men and women from African countries to serve with the Allied forces. They took part in campaigns in the Middle East, North Africa and East Africa, Italy and the Far East. Men of the 81st and 82nd West African Divisions served with great distinction against the Japanese in Burma, as part of the famous 'Forgotten' 14th Army. The 81st comprised units from the Gambia, Nigeria, Sierra Leone and the Gold Coast (now Ghana), while the 82nd comprised further reinforcements from Nigeria and the Gold Coast. Both Divisions formed part of the Royal West African Frontier Force (RWAFF). For years after the war Magba Kamara led the ex-servicemen's association and regularly attended the Cenotaph services on George Street.

I had a very good friend during that time, a well known former Royal Air Force (RAF) Officer by the name of Johnny Smythe. Born on 30th June 1915, in Freetown, when Britain declared war on Germany in 1939, Johnny volunteered to help in the war effort, and joined the RAF. He was one of only four, out of a batch of ninety men, to complete his training as an Officer. After spending another year studying to become a navigator, he joined a bomber squadron and later got promoted to Flying Officer. But on his 28th mission, on the night of 18th November

1943, his luck ran out. His bomber aircraft was flying at 16,000 ft when fighters came out of nowhere raking the fuselage with bullets and causing the pilot to order the crew to bail out. It seemed to Johnny to be the end as he parachuted to the ground, and hid in a barn. Some German soldiers who later raked the place with automatic fire couldn't believe their eyes. Johnny concluded that they could not come to terms with seeing a black man – and an officer at that, and they just stood there gazing in shock and amazement, which saved him from being shot immediately. After the war, Johnny studied law and returned to Sierra Leone where he became one of the leading lawyers in the country, and later took silk as a Queen's Counsel. Our friendship developed while I was working in the Masters Office of the Judicial Department, as a clerk to the Justices.

The general strike of 1955 proved to be a major event in that immediate post-war period. I witnessed it as a 10-year-old boy living in Congo Town, where Sissy (my mum) now managed Pa Davies's shop. On that memorable day, the strikers went into a rampage through the city, spreading to Congo Town. They looted Lebanese shops, destroyed several properties, street lights and caused widespread damage to the infrastructure. During the ensuing chaos, my family worried greatly about the safety of our shop. Fortunately, being a popular shop in the neighbourhood, the mob did not attack it. However, a local Lebanese businessman, at Westmoreland Street (now Siaka Stevens Street) caused a fatality when they looted his shop and he shot one rioter dead. He subsequently won an appeal against his sentence on the grounds of self-defence and provocation. The Commissioner of Police confirmed that he "shot to kill" in his attempt to restore civil order and rule of law in the city. The strike ended soon after, and from that time up to independence in 1961 there were no similar major strikes in the country.

The economy and trade soon returned to normal. Deep Water Quay at Cline Town, replaced Government Wharf as the main sea port. Ships from all over the world, including the major passenger liners – Accra, Aureol, Apapa from England and West African countries would dock in Freetown. Offices of various shipping companies, such as Elder Dempster Lines were all located at Cline Town. Seamen had abundant work, and people made the most of the available employment. We enjoyed a solid infrastructure in the country with a regular supply of electricity for those who could afford it. Those who couldn't afford to pay for electricity kept their sophisticated oil lamps and lanterns burning. People were content with their lifestyle and you never heard about anyone buying their own electrical generators in Sierra Leone until the Siaka Stevens and Momoh eras.

The next major infrastructural achievement in Sierra Leone, the Guma Valley reservoir and dam, constructed in the western mountains near a place called Lakkah, proved exciting. The massive pipeline ran right across Freetown, and took ages to lay. This major infrastructural project also provided lots of employment for people; we considered it a masterpiece of engineering in those days. We also had an eighteen-inch gauge railway network which covered some parts of the country. People were able to travel on it with produce such as pepper and cola nuts from their farms in the hinterland to the markets in Freetown. Relics of the main terminal for the railways in Freetown can still be seen at the other end of Wallace-JohnsonStreet in the area where the present Sierratel (formerly SLET) is now located. The earlier mountain railway system that ran up the hill to Wilberforce and Hill Station is a distant memory to most people of my generation.

We also had a good bus transportation system operated by the Road Transport Department. The main depots were at Cline Town and Oxford Street (now Lightfoot-Boston Street). Major roads were constructed to enable buses to penetrate deep into the provinces. Bus and railway routes were always very busy with people travelling on business or to pursue petty trading. At first we had what were known as "Bone-shaker" buses from Britain, then these were slowly replaced by modern Mercedes Benz buses from Germany. Double-decker buses were also a common sight in those days. All villages had buses and there were also buses going to all the main towns of the provinces. For the Freetown double-decker buses, the main route was from Cline Town to Congo Cross. All the major schools in Freetown had special buses for transporting children to and from school, including my own Collegiate School. I believe that we took our sound infrastructure for granted, and would be shocked in latter years at the loss of certain aspects of it like the railway network, and regular availability of electricity.

At this time, the nation enjoyed a rich social and cultural life. Freetown life was electric and buzzing, with many forms of entertainment, including our African culture and dance, which I enjoyed very much. A leading personality in this sector was John Akar.Born in 1927 at Rotifunk,

Bumpe Chiefdom, Moyamba District, in the Southern Province, to an Sherbro mother and a Lebanese father, he attended the local E.U.B School and subsequently, he went on to attend the Albert Academy in Freetown, before proceeding to the United States and Britain to continue his studies. Whilst abroad, he distinguished himself as a scholar, and a versatile communicator and entertainer. He studied commercial radio and television in America, Britain, France and the West Indies, and appeared on television and in films. In 1960, he became the first indigenous Director of Broadcasting and during his tenure, brought creative programme leadership to the Sierra Leone Broadcasting Service.

Akar succeeded in raising broadcasting to the highest professional standards that became the envy of the region. His aim was to get the Sierra Leone Broadcasting Service to reflect more and more the true image of the country, its music, its songs and its talent. He commanded much influence in these areas - he composed the tune of the Sierra Leone National Anthem to go with words written by C.N.Fyle. Logie E. Wright did the musical arrangement.

John Akar founded the National Dance Troupe, and used it as a vehicle to encourage Sierra Leoneans to be proud of their rich cultural heritage. He led the troupe on many successful performances around the world. After the Troupe's participation in the 1964 New York World Fair, the closing report stated: "This talented folk dance troupe imposed a vivid image of Sierre Leone on the minds of thousands of Americans when it took the New York World's Fair by storm in 1964". In fact, they were presented with a gold plaque after being voted the best dance ensemble at the Fair. In 1965, the Troupe performed at the Commonwealth Arts Festival in London, where it was a great success. The following year, the Troupe performed at the Festival of Negro Arts in Dakar, after which they did a four month tour of Western Europe.

The pioneering role played by John Akar awakened cultural consciousness among rural as well as urban populations, and firmly established Sierra Leone's place on the world cultural map. The immense potentialities of our indigenous cultures to rouse the people to action, cement national unity, and to open out to the wonderful realities of our times had been dormant. If there is one thing that John Akar achieved for his countrymen, it is that he managed to instill in them a sense of pride, a love for country and an awareness of our rich cultural heritage.

I was lucky to grow up when there were very high standards of education at every level right across the country. Freetown had a population of about 70 000 at the time, so schools were not overcrowded and could provide some good education. There were kindergartens and primary schools, but above all we had a bunch of excellent secondary schools. Bo School had been established for the education of the sons of chiefs, and the Harford Girls school in Moyamba catered for the girls of the Protectorate. The British Church Missionary Society had established the CMS Grammar School together with the Annie Walsh Memorial School, the Catholic Church ran the St Edwards School for boys, and St. Joseph's Convent School for girls, funny that because a convent is just that – a school for girls, the Albert Academy, the Methodist Boys High School, my school the Collegiate School, and the government run school of The Prince of Wales at King Tom. These schools were vibrant with pupils who were keen to excel at the Cambridge 'O' and 'A' level exams and we would engage in debates, quiz competitions and other academic activities in our smart school uniforms. Our boys and girls interacted well together, including writing letters to start courtships. One would write; "Perambulating in the streets of Freetown yesterday, I caught sight of your magnificent beauty!" The girls loved it, and felt rather special.

The excellence of tertiary education offered in Sierra Leone spread across the whole of West Africa. For learning and education, what can I say about our Fourah Bay College (FBC), University of Sierra Leone? Founded on February 18, 1827 as an Anglican missionary school by the CMS and now a public university in the neighbourhood of Mount Aureol in Freetown, this oldest university in West Africa, and the first western-style university in the region is quite famous. Formerly affiliated with Durham University in the UK (1876-1967), it is now a constituent college of the University of Sierra Leone.

The FBC soon became a magnet for the Creoles and other Africans seeking higher education under the British Empire, especially in the fields of theology and education. During our Colonial days, Freetown earned the nickname of "Athens of Africa" as an homage to the college. The first black principal of the university was an African-American missionary, Reverend Edward Jones from South Carolina in the United States. Lamina Sankoh was a prominent early academic. Students from most West African countries, mainly Nigeria, Ghana, Gambia, Cameroon and other

African countries were all rushing to Fourah Bay College to study. Yet even with our own tertiary institution many of my friends aspired to travelling overseas to England, America and Germany to gain degrees in faculties not available at the FBC, such as Engineering, Medicine and Law. The prospects of such experience in the wider world served to motivate us, and to shape our discussions and aspirations. We thoroughly enjoyed our education and immersed ourselves in learning.

But it was certainly not a case of 'all work and no play.' There were lots of places of entertainment, and fun. As ever, nightlife was booming in the east end, with lots of night clubs including a jazz club owned by a young prominent lawyer, Philo Jones. In the west end you had Gooding's Hall near King Jimmy market and the popular Wilberforce Memorial hall where social functions, and school dances were held. At Kroo Town Road, there were the famous Dworzak Hall and also the Blackstar Club owned by a famous Sierra Leone footballer called Gbatieh Davies, alias "Agbani". In Congo Town, there were famous bars such as "Odofo" owned by a Mr Kato Cole who was also a building contractor. West of Congo Town, not far from "Four-Road" was Pa Davies's bar, which my mum, Sissy managed. This popular bar in Congo Town, attracted some members of the Freetown elite, including popular lawyers in town, like the late Justice Ken During and Teddy Wyndham, a lawyer working for the Crown Law Office. We had departmental shops like CFAO, a French company, operating in Freetown, with everything for sale in those days. They also owned A Genet & CO, Cold Storage and Multi-Stores on the then Oxford Street.

Sports, mainly in the form of cricket, athletics and football, were superb in the 50s and 60s. The main football stadium at that time was located at King Tom. There were three divisions. Most of the secondary boys' schools in Freetown had teams in all three divisions. Leading Division One clubs included Railway, East End Lions, Ports Authority from the East End of Freetown and from the West End of Freetown were Mighty Blackpool, Prince of Wales, Richmond, Regents Olympic, Albert Academy, Old Edwardians, St Anthony's and Barmeh. The military fielded the Frontier Rangers, and the police force had their team, not to mention United African Company (U.A.C.), a subsidiary of Unilever who fielded a good team being a big employer; their captain, Hassan Bangurah, also found time to become a celebrated artist. C.F.A.O had a team in the 1st division, known as Washington, comprising mostly French men but including Samura Sesay who later turned politician. Bamin Brothers and the Benjamin Brothers from Sawpit in Central Freetown formed Santos, a good team that got promoted to Division 1. Two of their leading players were Wallace Kargbo, alias the "Wizard" and Prince Elba (ex-Collegiate School boy).

My own school, Collegiate did not have a team but nonetheless produced talented footballers who played for leading clubs. Ex president Momoh played for Mighty Blackpool, when they were called Blackpool FC, and he was very good. To give him credit, he contributed a lot towards football in Freetown. After he stopped playing, he became president of Mighty Blackpool sports club. I was his Assistant Secretary.

I must take time to pay a short tribute to footballers who helped to develop the game. Among them were:

Lamini, Alpha Dondoli, Abu Wilson (playing for Railway) Amadu Kamara alias "Okrol" and Omassa Kamara both ex-Collegiate school pupils (playing for east End Lions) Bami Ashman and Jalloh (playing for Albert Academy) Frederick Pratt, Kassim, Donald George, Lamin, Joe Sesay (the youngest) Roland Warne, Septimus Kai-Kai (all playing for Regent Olympic). Their goalkeeper then was Jah Tucker, succeeded by Billy Jones, also a national cricketer. John Kiester played for Regent Olympic. You had Boye Davies, Kester-Campbell who later became a politician, and Kapindi Jamiru who became a top civil servant, and a Government Minister, and also played for Richmond (Methodist Boys High School).

And now an extra-special tribute to my team Mighty Blackpool. Before the days of Kama Dumbuya, you had players like Edward Akar, Weah Sawyerr, Tamba Kamara, alias "Stanley Matthews" who also later turned politician in the APC government under Siaka Stevens and Momoh. Two brothers also played for "Mighty Blackpool" at this time: Sylvanus Morris and Kobinah Morris. Sallu Jalloh, goalkeeper extraordinaire, followed Mohammed Turay of Prisons and East End Lions fame as our second national goalkeeper. Other star players were the legendary Boye Johnson and the deadly duo of Juleh Peters and Dedeh Bangura. The best-loved players for Blackpool during this period were Weah Sawyerr and Saidu J Momoh. He remained a good centre half back and from a good family until Siaka Stevens brought him into politics. Weah Sawyerr became a respectable church minister. During this period the famous Ahmed Brothers of Congo Town managed Blackpool. They were succeeded by the Basma Brothers, famous Lebanese businessmen of Kissy Street and under the Presidency of Saidu J Momoh. I played occasionally in the second division team before I became the Assistant Secretary. Later on in the 60s the club had great players like Samuel Kamara, Abdullah "Garincha" Sesay, Ola George, Boye Johnson, Kama Dumbuya, Samuel Wesley, Collins Thomas, and Conton Sesay alias Aberdeen Pele. Blackpool, as I am made to understand, is still dominating football in Sierra Leone these days. Justice won't be done if I don't pay tribute to James Cole that prolific and versatile player for the Police football team in the late 50s.

In the field of athletics, most secondary schools held their own sports day events at the Recreation Grounds at Brookfields, except for the Prince of Wales school who held theirs at their school grounds at King Tom. The grand schools' athletics competitions were held at the Recreation Grounds in which secondary schools would compete against each other for trophies. The competitions were fierce! The Police Force held their own athletics meeting annually with different units competing against each other at their grounds in King Tom barracks; the military force held theirs at their grounds at Wilberforce military barracks. These were all good occasions and as a young teenager I always looked forward to these great sporting events. I also looked forward to, and attended, the Boxing Day sports, open to all athletes in the country. These featured people competing for prize money and trophies. I always looked forward to watching competitors climbing the greasy pole, to retrieve a sack full of money at the top. Competitors would get to the top of the pole by the end of the day, but this required teamwork. Other main attractions were the cycle race, the relay, and the 400 metres, and spectators were thrilled to watch cycling at its best. Champion cyclists included riders like the Benjamin Brothers, the Bamin Brothers, William Kamara of Murray Town, Julius Davies of Congo Town, and "Borbor Waitman".

Finally, we could look forward to the Queen's Birthday Parade, a military ceremony with the Changing of the Guards held at the Recreation Grounds, as another great social occasion. Before Independence and immediately after, our Army was called the Royal Sierra Leone Military Force (RSLMF) under the Command of Brigadier Blackie, the last Englishman to act as Force Commander before handing over to our own Brigadier David Lansana. After the main parade, there followed a match past of different organisations such as schools – secondary and primary, obviously in their colourful uniforms, Red Cross, Boys Brigades, Boy Scouts, Girl Guides, Police Force, Fire Force, Coast Guards; Women's Organisations, Ex-Servicemen Association, led by their late President Mr. Magba Kamara. We experienced Sierra Leone at her best before deterioration set in.

John Akar

Flying Officer Johnny Smythe RAF

Chapter 5

Our first coup

Sierra Leone became Independent from the UK in 1961, but In 1967–8 struggled under military rule, following a coup. The country became a Republic in 1971, with a presidential form of government. In 1978 it became a one-party State, under the All People's Congress who abolished the post of Prime Minister. I believe that this period of coups and counter coups with several gruesome executions of many remarkable nation building sons of the soil represented a real blot on our history, only to be surpassed years later in 1991 when we became embroiled in a particularly brutal civil war lasting for eleven years.

During the regime of Sir Albert Margai, in 1964, as a teenager attending the Collegiate Secondary School at Wilkinson Road in Freetown, I came across the former Major Ambrose Ghanda and his English wife taking a stroll on the road behind the school. Immediately he recognised me and we greeted each other and started chatting. He said to me,

"Are you attending this school"?

My reply was, "Yes sir". Although not in the military myself, I gave him that honour and respect.

"This is my favourite school" he went on. "Are you still playing football?"

"Yes, sir" I replied; "I am in the school's first squad".

"I won't be surprised," he said. We chatted, and he recalled his earlier days at Murray Town Barracks, when we frequently played football matches at the depot, most of the time playing against the leading teams in the military. The military had star players: people like K.P. Davies, Abu Noah, Joseph Saidu Momoh, Amadu Kargbo, and playing with such proved risky because those men played with great physical strength, and we did not have the protection of yellow and red cards, and were left in the hands of God. My mother used to say, "You will die on the football grounds with all this pain you accumulate in your body".

I virtually grew up at Murray Town barracks and worst of all, my mother Janet, used to cook food for the Murray Town barracks primary school children. The headmistress, a very nice lady called Mrs Cynthia Shooter, grew up and attended school with my mother in Hastings. In fact she had helped my mother secure the job. I am not sure whether nepotism is always a bad thing as people invariably helped each other along, giving 'a leg up' to friends and family in our society....it seemed the only way to survive.

I first had contact with the military when we were at Congo Town around 1956, as a pupil of the Murray Town primary school. I became very ill and a young English Lieutenant helped me to get medical attention. He lived in a very nice bungalow a few hundred yards from us, and would come regularly to us for his supplies. Sometimes, I would assist with carrying his items to his house. We became friends, and one day when I became ill, he sent the driver with his Land Rover to collect me, and take me to the military barracks hospital at Wilberforce, known as '34'. There, I started to receive treatment for my kidney, and they would collect me and bring me back home. But this illness could not be diagnosed properly with a reliable prognosis, and the problem stayed with me until later on in my life.

Meanwhile, the politics of the country continued to develop all around us, and people were very anxious. At Independence, Albert's half-brother, Sir Milton Margai was appointed first Prime Minister of Sierra Leone with Albert serving as a Member of Parliament for Moyamba. Albert received a Roman Catholic education at St Edward's Primary School and went on to be one of the first group of students to attend St Edward's Secondary School. He worked as a registered nurse from 1931 to 1944, and later travelled to England to read law at the Inner Temple, Inns of Court, where he qualified in 1948. Prior to his political career, he owned a private law practice in Freetown.

Margai was a founder member of the Sierra Leone National Party, which was formed in 1949 to advocate and aid in the transition to Independence for the country. However, in the years leading up to Independence, he associated more closely with Siaka Stevens than his brother. He took leadership of the Sierra Leone People's Party (SLPP) in 1957, but stepped down to form the People's National Party (PNP) with Stevens. A major point of contention between the two groups involved the degree of involvement of traditional chiefs and traditional rulers in the modern state. In fact, Margai openly asked traditional rulers to stay out of politics. He became one of a number of leaders such as Kwame Nkrumah in Ghana, and Milton Obote in Uganda who attempted to remove the system of democratic governance enshrined in multi-party democracy as he believed that this would encourage politicians to accentuate the ethnic differences within the state, and therefore threaten the viability of Sierra Leone as a country. When I look at the situation in the country today, and the debilitating effect tribalism has in our society, one has to say he could have been right.

In 1961, even though I had started at Collegiate school at Wilkinson Road, my real ambition was to join the Military school at Juba. I would have been amongst the first set of boys to start at that school. Regrettably, I could not pass the physical exam to get in. Nevertheless, I was always with those boys, several of whom became my friends. Through that close association with people in the military, I got to know that John Bangura and Ambrose Ghanda were suspended from the Army because officials discovered a plot that they wanted to overthrow the government. When Sir Albert discovered that the two officers were plotting to overthrow his government, he suspended them from the army, and eventually sent them out of the country. Bangura went to New York as a representative of the government and Ambrose Ghanda ended up in Moscow as Sierra Leone's ambassador.

On being appointed Minister of Finance in 1962, Margai proceeded to change Sierra Leone's currency from the British pound to the 'leone', a decimal legal tender equivalent to half a sterling pound at the time. He also founded the Bank of Sierra Leone, and made it the national bank. More importantly, Albert Margai became Prime Minister on 29 April 1964 attracting lots of criticism during his tenure. He had a liking for extravagant pageantry and was accused of corruption, and of a policy of affirmative action in favour of the Mende tribe. The tantrum-prone Prime Minister inherited the nicknamed "Akpata". Above all, he endeavoured to change Sierra Leone from a democracy to a one-party state. Up until the 1967 elections, Sierra Leone had been an exemplary democratic, post-colonial state. However, the campaign strategies of Margai would forever alter this trend. He objected to any candidates from the opposition running against candidates from his own party. Margai refused to dignify accusation of corruption with a response. Riots broke out across Sierra Leone and the government had to declare a state of emergency. These were becoming troubled times.

Neither Margai nor his opponent, Siaka Stevens, achieved a clear majority in the 1967 elections. Brigadier David Lansana, the Commander of Sierra Leone's Armed Forces at the time, therefore arrested and detained the Governor-General Sir Henry Lightfoot -Boston, Sir Albert Margai and Siaka Stevens. He declared martial law, dismissed the election results, and proclaimed himself the interim head of state, and The Chief Justice C.O.E Cole became the Caretaker of the Constitution of the Country. Colonel Ambrose Ghanda was in Russia as our Ambassador so also was Major John Bangura as our representative in United States of America these 2 military men were got rid of out of the Country in an earlier coup plot which was leaked. to overthrow Sir Albert.

Whilst this chaos was going on, another group of Senior officers, namely, Charles Blake, Major Jumu and others,stepped in and arrested Brigadier David Lansana announcing on the radio that they had taken over the Government because they believed, and suspected that David Lansana's true intention was to declare Sir Albert Margai as the winner of the elections, and install him as Prime Minister.

However, in April 1968, a group of 8 non-commissioned officers staged a counter coup in an attempt to restore the democratic process to Sierra Leone. Thus, Sierra Leone got its fifth government in a week, which set a new record even for restless Africa. The actual change had taken place while Lt. Colonel Ambrose Patrick Ghanda, 39, was on British United Airways Flight 321 from London to Freetown after being summoned from Russia to head the new military junta. Also on the plane was Col. Juxon-Smith. The junta had cabled their first choice, Lt. Colonel. Ambrose Ghanda, to remain at his post, but he had already reached London on his way home. On arrival home, Brigadier Juxon-Smith was appointed Leader of the National Reformation Council (NRC).

After the so-called Sergeants Coup, the National Reformation Council elected Brigadier John Bangura to the post of Head of State. Bangura, who was not politically ambitious, served briefly from April 18, 1968 to April 22, 1968. A staunch democrat, he then re-instated Siaka Stevens because he had won the election. Bangura arrested every high-ranking officer in the army and police, so that he could restore the constitution and democracy to Sierra Leone. Margai warned: "If the Stevens government does not do something to elevate the lives of the have-nots, the poor, they would one day rise to demand from the haves, the rich, their own share of the economy." On 18 December 1980, Margai died peacefully in his sleep not realising how his words were going to come to pass some eleven years later in a brutal civil war.

Earlier, when I first met Colonel Ghanda after he was suspended from the army before he left for Moscow, he resided at the back of Collegiate school, in a very nice house with his family, once occupied by Desmond Luke and then later by Dr Marcus-Jones, my mother's lawyer. These were both popular lawyers in Freetown. I saw Colonel Ghanda and we chatted casually, but what brought me even closer to him were his pets. He had three boa constrictors in cages, and a deer. Animals and their behaviour always fascinated me. Even today, 'wildlife' presented by David Attenborough is one of my favourite programmes on television. It gives me so much pleasure, excitement, to learn about other living things on our planet earth.

As I mentioned earlier, I had known Ambrose Ghanda in Murray Town barracks. Little did I know, after many years, that I was to meet him again in London. This happened after the overthrow of the Momoh government by Captain Valentine Strasser and other officers. Over the years, people were convinced that Momoh and the APC government proved to be very reckless and irresponsible after Siaka Stevens. Sierra Leoneans all over the world were jubilant. The UK Diaspora organised a very peaceful and jubilant demonstration at the Sierra Leone High Commission, London, in Portland Place to rejoice for the redemption of our country from selfish and corrupt people and thuggery. Strasser, a few months later, ordered that political parties should resume their activities. The Sierra Leone People's Party (SLPP) UK branch re-emerged. Meetings were held at the Lambeth Town Hall in Brixton to start recruiting members. For me I had always been drawn to that party, and my friend Ambrose Ganda, who had become a lawyer in London, spoke to me wanting me to take an active role in the party for the future. I always respected him as I felt that he had good intentions for his country. In fact, Siaka Stevens made several attempts to bring Ganda into his government but was turned down repeatedly. Ambrose Ganda and Siaka Stevens did not have the same ideology in politics. Little did I know that Ambrose was secretly campaigning on my behalf to be elected as the party branch secretary in London.

On Election Day at the Lambeth Town Hall, we had a full house. Among those present were the late Mrs Cummings-John, Colonel Ghanda, and my good old friend and political activist Ambrose Ganda. Candidates introduced themselves and we elected Mr John Saad as Party Chairman, UK branch. He was quite good. Miss Hawa Kallon was appointed secretary while I was elected assistant secretary. She was quite good and we worked closely with members in Sierra Leone, contributing towards policy-making for the party.

At the same time the SLPP in Sierra Leone selected their officials and party leader; finally, Mr Ahmed Tejan Kabba was elected as leader. For me, this was welcome news. I was convinced that this was a good choice. He held high office in Sir Albert's government and also in Juxon-Smith's government. He also served in the United Nations African development Team. He had all the qualities and experience to become a good leader. On a personal connection, he was married to my late cousin, Patricia, Miss Pat, as we used to call her. So, in these circumstances I was going to put a special effort to raise the profile of SLPP in London.

After our election meeting I went over to Colonel Ghanda, to introduce myself. But, much to my surprise, he did not quite recollect who I was. How sad, and peculiar; so we just spoke generally about the meeting and the election. I never saw him again after that.

Chapter 6

Class 66

I feel proud and privileged to have attended the West African Methodist Collegiate Secondary School for boys, which has produced so many great men like Wallace - Johnson, that great journalist and politician. In fact, he turned out to be a very good friend of my grandfather, Christopher Williams. with whom he settled in Congo - Brazzaville in the 1920s.

My father had always talked about sending me to Bo Secondary School in the Southern District of Sierra Leone, that august seat of learning fit for the sons of chiefs,or to Albert Academy in Freetown, He frequently talked about the town of Bo. I can recall the day he even took me to the school, a visit coinciding with their inter-house athletics sports event. I liked the visit, and at the end became convinced that I would attend that secondary school when I grew up. But my destiny took me to Collegiate School instead, and I loved every minute of it from day one, until 1966 when I graduated.

Collegiate school was a great school, full of discipline and lots of great teachers with great characters. The principal himself ,Pa Garber, as we used to call him, taught Greek and Latin. The vice-principal. Pa King, as we called him, covered Geography. Willie Pratt was exceptionally good in Science, especially in Biology and Chemistry. Pa Thomas, alias "Master" and Mr. Edwin, were famous for Latin and Literature. The latter, who later joined the army and became an Education Officer, was a great sports man as well. He spent all his resources managing a great first division football team, St Anthony.

Pa Willie doubled up as the English teacher and choirmaster. Mrs Caroline Roy-Macaulay and Helen French both taught Geography; Mr Willie Young, Solomon Tucker, and Mr. Koroma taught Physics and Maths; Francis Minah and Mr. Webber taught Maths; Margaret Manley taught Literature; Pa Smith, alias "Albayeah" taught geography; Pa Spain and Mr. Kanu taught English and Literature; Mr Roland Timity taught Maths and Religious Knowledge; Mr Nichols taught History. For us, the greatest and most notorious was Pa Decker who called himself "Congo Decker" for a reason unknown to me. These teachers were involved in what I would call the front line teaching of the class of 66 and made an impact on all of us students.

This was a tough class. You could either be brilliant academically or be very good at sports. For example we had the great Manneh Peters, my personal friend, who went on to play for the Sierra Leone national football team and also became a national coach. He was such a gifted footballer. I always considered him to be like the great Cubilas of Peru. Other great players included Dixon Koroma, Collins MacFoy, and William Momoh, the younger brother of the future President Momoh. We also had three other sets of brothers in the same class, including Alfred and Raymond George, the former becoming a member of parliament and the younger a lecturer at the University of Sierra Leone. Other classmates included Idrissa Iscandri, Alfred Kamara and Victor Cole from Murray Town, Aaron and George Johnson, Umaru Sesay, Tamba Aiah from Kono, Alfred Tokumbor Wilson,

Mohammed Njai from Gambia, David Easmond; Ahmed Aboki from Nigeria; Mustapha Hassan, Bunting Davies from Aberdeen Village;,Willie Parsons, Hudson Lawson from Regent Village, not forgetting the Benjamin Brothers Edmett and Ayo, David Wakka, Samuel Walker and the great Thomas Fraser, both from Murray Town. The latter became Cabinet Secretary and later Permanent Secretary; Richard During, now a US Attorney. Samuel Wyse was our pianist at the morning assembly. In fact ,we had two excellent pianists for assembly : Samuel Wyse and Hudson Lawson (now a senior government pharmacist). I also remember Momodu Mansaray;,Ade Victor Jones, Sonny Joe, Leonard Kamara, Abel Sawyer, Victor During, Gaston Brown, David Johnston, Ernest Johnson,Jacob Spain-Cole, Monzul Swarray, and Simeon Campbell. All these students went on to be great achievers either as academics, or as sportsmen.

As for me, I almost made it at soccer. I had the opportunity to excel and establish myself as one of the leading up-coming goalkeepers in Freetown but I threw it away with just one blunder. The years 1964 -1966 were excellent years for Collegiate School in soccer. In 1964 we won the Secondary School championship, with players like Manneh Peters, Dixon Koroma, Maxim Bright, Collins Macfoy, the Benjamin Brothers, Ishmael Koroma, Mohamed "Fangay Juju", to name just a few of these players.

Our main football rival was St Edwards Secondary School, which was also in the National League. That team had great players like Patrick Kemokai, Pat Sowe, Dangawali in goal, and Bangura alias "Bangso". These were all great players who went on to play in the national side. Another rival team was Independent Memorial School. It had Frank Williams in goal. He went on to play for the great East End Lions football team, and was also the national goalkeeper. Also in their team was my friend McCarthy from Congo Town, who also played for the prison football club.

The final for the schools league in 1966 was between Collegiate and Independent – I played in goal for Collegiate and Frank Williams kept goal for Independent. This game was played twice, the first being at the Police Grounds, King Tom. This first match had to be abandoned, as fighting erupted in the grounds. The Police had to disperse the crowd with tear gas. It was not a wonderful sight. Later, it was decided we had to replay the match to determine the champion. This time it was at the Prince of Wales School grounds at King Tom. This second match was violence-free. Both our principal, Mr Victor Hastings-Spaine, and the games master, M. S. Turay had given us a strict warning prior to the game to comport ourselves well. Both teams fielded more or less the same squad as in the first game, including Frank in their goal and myself in ours. With fifteenminutes gone, Ishmael Koroma registered our first and what was to be the winning goal. Manneh Peters, "Fangay Juju", Dixon Koroma, the Benjamin brothers, Maxim Bright, Collins Macfoy were at their best. At half-time Collegiate still was leading one-nil. With only minutes to the end of the match, a penalty was awarded in favour of Independent. Our winning the championship now depended on me to save the penalty; a draw would mean Independent winning the championship. This was a do or die moment for me, and I really was determined to prevent a goal. Spectators and players were all tense. McCarthy was going to take the penalty. I watched his eyes and recognised which direction he wanted to kick the ball. I was right; I saved it and we won the championship! For the years 1964 through 1966 the two national coaches then, Patrick Kamara and Frederick Pratt, were monitoring my performance in goal for my school and they also watched me regularly when I practised with my team, Mighty Blackpool.

My big break came when they decided to include me in the full squad for the Western Area Secondary Schools against the team comprising Northern Province Secondary Schools. Our team was magnificent. I was privileged to have been selected as goalkeeper over Frank Williams of Independent School and Dangawali of St Edwards School. The rest of the squad included Pat Sowe, Prince Elba, Manneh Peters, Patrick Kemokai, Mohammed "Fangay Juju", Dixon Koroma. We spent the day at the Albert Academy School before the match and by 4 p.m. we left in a brand new Mercedes Benz bus for the Recreational Grounds at Brookfields. By that time the stadium was packed. The guest of honour was the Prime Minister, Sir Albert Margai, accompanied by a few other ministers.

Our team was great, but fifteen minutes into the game, I allowed an easy goal. This greatly demoralised our squad. It was such a terrible blunder and the situation, compared today, was similar to that involving David Seaman, the England goalkeeper in the 2002 World Cup against Brazil. Before that match, the English were saying he was one of the best goalkeepers in the world; after that match the English crowd hated him!

In 1965 I was in the same predicament as David Seaman. However, before the end of the first half, we equalised.

Patrick Kamara and Frederick Pratt insisted that I should remain in the goal after the blunder. I was determined not to let in another goal. My confidence and motivation grew. Even though I made several spectacular saves, they defeated us 2-1. A section of the crowd was hostile against me and they could have hurt me. At the end of the game I could not even wait for the presentation by the Prime Minister. A pair of Adidas football boots was given to each player in the losing team. Because of the hostility of the crowd and seeing that I was in potential danger, S. B. Mara came to my rescue and sneaked me away from the crowd; put me in his white Mercedes Benz and took me home to Byrne Lane. I was devastated.

We sat for a while as he tried to comfort and encourage me. Since then we became good friends. I came to like and admire him. He would visit me regularly in Byrne Lane. I found him to be a very downtoearth individual as our friendship grew. Later he fell in love with one of my cousins, and married her.

S.B. Mara was one of two parliamentarians I liked in those days, the other being Manah Kpaka. He was one of the politicians in Sierra Leone who, after the 1967 fiasco when the SLPP under Sir Albert Margai fell from power, never ran away from the country. He appeared before commissions of inquiry and was never implicated in any form of corruption. He stayed quietly in the country, opened his travel agency business, Alitalia, and was content without any trouble. In fact, he was even given a ministerial position under Siaka Stevens's All People's Congress government. This came as a surprise to me, as S. B. was a die-hard S.L.P.P member, but as a leader Stevens was always full of political ploys.

For me, that game in which I was the western area goalkeeper was nearly the end of my football career. In fact, a few days after that game we had to play St Edwards School at the Association Grounds, King Tom. I swore never to play again because I was ashamed of my previous performance. Collins Macfoy, Manneh Peters, the Benjamin Brothers, and the whole Collegiate squad had confidence in me and persuaded me to play and not to give up. I yielded, and once again I was in good shape. It ended 0 – 0 and all the Edwards players including Pat Sowe, Patrick Kemokai, and "Bangso" came up to me and congratulated me for a brilliant goalkeeping display, and asked me,

"What went wrong on that day?"

I replied, "it was one of those days".

By that time my sister Koryeh was in England. She had promised me that if I worked hard she would send for me to proceed to England for further studies. I accepted this challenge. This meant that I had to cut down on playing football, turning my attention to acting as Assistant Secretary for the Mighty Blackpool football club. At the same time Momoh had just been made a Brigadier and was made the President of the club, before he entered into politics. Up until then we were good friends. While in England, I tried to correspond with him when he was made President of the country, (more in regard to the club Mighty Blackpool). I was toying with the idea of getting in touch with manufacturers of football shirts and boots at discount prices. I did not get any response from him. He couldn't say he did not get the letter because it was his Inspector-general of police, Bambay Kamara, a friend of my family, who took the letter and handed it to him. He did not reply of course, because politics may have gone to his head too much. He forgot the little friends he grew up with, seemingly just as Ganda did also.

Long live my beloved Collegiate School. "Collegiate Rah! Rah! Rah! "

Collegiate School after winning the schools championship with Games Master MS Turay(r) and late Principal MA Garber (c) and Vice-Principal Victor Hastings-Spaine. Author in the foreground (w ball)

Mighty Blackpool football team, just before a Division One game against East End Lions at Association Grounds, Kingtom. I (deputy goalkeeper) am at the extreme right - back row

Chapter 7

On to employment

Soon, my school days were over. I had studied quite hard to take the London GCSE and had a C grade in RE and General Principles of English, but this left no possibility of going on to 'A' levels. I, therefore, embarked on a brief period as a working man in Freetown.

Initially, I worked for about nine months as a health assistant at a government clinic at Cline Town, giving vaccinations before issuing the World Health Organization certificates. I got this job through my lifelong friend, Dr. Marcella Davies, Senior Medical Officer at the clinic. She is the daughter of the late Mr. Davies, owner of the shop at Congo Cross which my mother managed. They trained me to give vaccinations, sign a section of the certificate, and then forward the certificate to Dr. Davies who gave the inoculation before signing and issuing the certificate to the patient. I did not particularly like this job, but at least it earned me some money, and I met lots of people. Above all, I dreaded the sight of Mr. Kojo Hamilton, the recruiting manager for the shipping agencies, who would arrive with about twenty to fifty newly-recruited seafarers that had to be vaccinated and given certificates. I sometimes felt sorry for Dr. Marcella Davies who too had to do her own part of the process. However, we were obliged to provide these essential services, and I benefitted from this much-needed exposure to the real working world.

At the end of the nine months assignment at the clinic, I stayed home for a few weeks before securing another job at the diamond factory at Pultney Street. In that factory they specialised in cutting, shaping and polishing the stones. The company exercised the strictest security; once you clocked in and entered the building in the morning, you were not allowed to venture outside until it the end of the working day. The company provided food for us twice a day. I was a trainee diamond polisher, and my trainer and supervisor was a man called Lawrence Myers, very brilliant at his job. He took particular interest in me when he got to know that I was a friend and neighbour to his sister, Elsie May Kallon, at Byrne Lane, Aberdeen Ferry Road. So, even at this early age as an adult I began to experience the advantage of knowing the right people in a society without agencies that would serve that purpose. Sadly, this dependency on nepotism invariably engenders bribery and corruption.

Working as a trainee diamond polisher proved a high risk and sensitive job. If you were assigned twenty diamond stones to polish in the morning, you had to account for the same twenty diamonds at the end of the day. One problem we encountered was that it was easy for a piece of diamond to come out of the loop and fall on the floor. You then had the arduous task of sweeping the whole factory floor, collecting the dirt on one side at the end of the room, put it through a sieve and try to find the diamond. During the next three months, I had to do this about three times. Luckily, I found my diamonds so I never got into trouble, but I always dreaded that one day I wouldn't be so lucky. With this constant fear in me, I one day took my overall, went to Mr. Myers and told him that I wished to leave the job as it had become too stressful for me. Mr Myers tried to dissuade me, saying that I was doing just fine. I then told him that in my constant state of anxiety I might lose a diamond one day, so I had decided to leave. It was quite a relief for me to move on!

My big break came in January 1968 when I started working in the Masters Office, Law Courts, as a clerical officer. I felt great. The Master of Court, Mr. Omrie Golley had Mrs. Virginia Wright as his deputy. Very few people knew the Senior Registrar, Mr R. A. Woode, as a good friend of our family, but I knew that I got the job through his influence: almost a reverse case of 'who knows you!' Mr, Woode assumed my mentorship, teaching me most of the job and all the risky part of it, especially taking care of 'case files' which were to be kept under lock and key. Sometimes, high risk case files were kept in a locked safe. I worked with very good colleagues like Alex Kamara, Thomas Bright, Egbert Thomas, Moses Reffell, Mrs. Johnson, Victor Horton, Fatmata Tarawalli, Mildred Cole, and Mrs. Khanga. For the first few weeks I worked in the office and slowly I started to attend court with judges presiding and lawyers prosecuting and defending. In those days you had prosecuting counsels like Mr. Adophy, P.P Kebbie, Decker, Kamal, Pierre Boston, Solomon Berewa, Mr. Bernard, and Claude Campbell. Later, when the treason trial involving Brigadier David Lansana and fourteen others started, the chief prosecuting counsel was Cyril Rogers-Wright. He had just been re-instated to the Bar after a long spell of suspension, and I witnessed his swearing in ceremony by Chief Justice C.O.E Cole.

Prominent practising lawyers in those days were Cyril Rogers-Wright, his son Cyrus Rogers-Wright, Dr Henry Joko–Smart, Desmond Luke, Mr Fashole Luke, Dr Marcus Jones, Doe Smith, Freddie Short, Francis M Minah, FM

Carew, Pa McCormack, Pa Mackay Senior, Ken During, Lawyer Basma, Lawyer Aboud, Mr. Riby Williams, Bunting Thompson, Mr Tejan Cole, Arnold Gooding, George Gelaga -King. Female lawyers included Miss Frances Wright, Mrs. Christine Harding, Miss Patricia Macaulay, and Mrs Agnes Macaulay née Momoh, who later became a formidable judge. As I listened to all these brilliant lawyers in court, I naturally started thinking seriously about a possible career in the law. I often imagined that one day I ,too, would stand up and argue in court, just like these learned men and women.

My main colleague and other mentor, Alex Kamara, was very conscientious and diligent in his work completed mainly in the criminal courts. As I began to develop self confidence in my work, I felt able to accompany a Jjdge to court, all by myself starting with Justice Donald Macaulay. Soon we developed a very good working relationship. At this time he often sat on civil cases. A very enterprising man off duty, he engaged in the unusual hobby of deep sea fishing. He was always very smartly dressed. Our office was just next door to his chambers. Most times after a court session ended and all the files had been put in order, he would come around to request a file and some law books which had been referenced in court pertaining to a case. He would read and make his judgement. When not sitting in court, he would sometimes come to my office and request that I accompany him to do some shopping. I was always very happy when I moved around with him as I felt it boosted my status to go around with an important personality in our small community. One day I accompanied him to shop at a store called Henry Duck, located at the then Oxford Street in Freetown, at the junction of Howe Street near Kingsway Stores. He always went there to buy oil for his speedboat, which he used for fishing. He had parked his car in the wrong place causing a traffic offence. I sat waiting for him in the car when a traffic policeman came and enquired of me who owned the vehicle. I told him the vehicle belonged to Justice Donald Macaulay. "Oh! Alright" he said. Just then Mr Macauley came out of the shop and spotted the policeman who had just finished talking to me. He came in the car and asked me, "What did that policeman say to you?"I said, "He told me you are parked on the wrong place and it's a traffic offence". His reply,

"Why didn't he book us?"

I have to say I could not quite determine whether he felt the policeman had failed in his duty to uphold the law regardless, or objected to any hint of favouritism. What was the bigger evil, inefficiency or nepotism? We drove off and he dropped me in front of the office.

"How many cases do we have tomorrow?"

"Three," I replied.

"Ok, see you in the morning.".

Apart from our official duties in court, Justice Macaulay'appeared to treat me as his quasi confidant. Although he had his driver called Saffa who also did little errands for him, I did most of the complicated ones, like going to the treasury to cash his claim vouchers when they came from the provinces where he sat on cases as a circuit judge. On my return from the treasury with his cash, he would sometimes "dash" me between £20- £30, this represented a pretty good change, as the exchange rate was two Leones (the local currency) to one British pound sterling. Unfortunately, it was after our hosting of the Organization of African Unity (OAU) summit that the currency began to take a dive. We began to see Presidents Stevens and Momoh printing their heads on our currency in the normal way, but as if to spell doom for our once valuable currency. Today it is beyond belief, that the echange rate is one British pound to over 6,000 Leones!

I supported Justice Macaulay in various and different ways. One day I felt so guilty after I turned down his request to accompany him on a weekend fishing trip for the simple reason that I couldn't swim. For me, growing up at Murray Town by the seaside, and not knowing how to swim was an embarrassment. I felt guilty when he would return from his fishing trips with big catches. I'm talking here about deep-sea fishing where his buyer was Freetown Cold Storage, Howe Street. I would take his monster catches, with Saffa driving of course, to do the price negotiation and sale, and return with his cheque.

By this time my sister Beatrice was busy making arrangements for me to travel to England to study. We tried earlier but because I had not received a letter of acceptance from Bolton Technical College to which I had applied, I could not get a visa to enter England. Around June 1971, after I paid a year's fee to the college, I got a letter of acceptance that pleased me immensely! Next, I had to re-apply for an entry certificate to travel to England.

I had no idea who to approach to help me. A few days later, Justice Macaulay called me during lunchtime after finishing in court to go shopping with him. We went to the usual shop to buy speedboat oil. After we finished the transactions I revealed the good news to him. That was the first time he knew about my plans to travel abroad to England, an idea he favoured immediately because he knew I would progress if I had the opportunity. I showed him my college letter of acceptance and my passport which I had with me. I then explained how I had been turned down for a visa previously by the strict consular officer at the British High Commission. He said, "give me your papers". From inside the shop he used their phone, this was before the age of mobile phones of course, and requested to speak to the Consular Officer at the High Commission.

"This is Justice Donald Macaulay here," he said in his quiet 'English' accent. "My court clerk, Mr Tucker is to go to England to start Bolton Technical College in September. He has got a letter of acceptance and he needs an entry certificate." He went on, "Don't you think it will be good for him to go by August so that he can begin to get used to the climate before he starts in September?"

The officer obviously agreed. I went and introduced myself, handed him my passport, letter from the college, and showed him a letter from my sister. He immediately approved my application, and granted me an entry certificate for a year, much to my relief. I called on my benefactor later in his chambers to show him my passport stamped with a visa to enter Britain; I said to him,

"I don't know how to thank you, Sir."

"That's alright" he said, "I will miss you very much when you go."

Next, I had to face working in the civil courts with Justice Rowland Harding; some thought he was a very difficult judge to work with normally. Most clerks who came down from the court vowed not to work with him again, and saw him as a no-nonsense judge. To show what I mean, one day while in court, a serious argument ensued between two leading counsels during a case involving property. One prominent Freetown lawyer had exceeded the limit in his legal argument. In the end, Justice Harding warned him that if he was not careful he would send him down for contempt. In the end, he never did. When I got to work with him, I found out that before each court session started I needed, first of all, to let him have the case files for the day so that he could have a brief before going to court. Secondly, he liked to see his court well staffed, for example, with bailiffs, a policeman, interpreter, and all the relevant books on hand, like law reports, and matrimonial clauses act. When lawyers made references to these books, the clerk had to find the relevant pages and tag them. These were the bread and butter requirements I needed to know to get along with him.

Most times when Justice Harding returned to his chambers he would send his usher to fetch me to talk about work. I remember we just completed a divorce case in which Cyrus Rogers-Wright acted as the respondent's lawyer. When the petitioner's lawyer was struggling to cite from the Matrimonial Clauses Act, Cyrus would help him out by completely reciting the Act without looking at the book and without error. Justice Harding said to me in his chambers,

"You see what I always tell you about Cyrus?"

"Yes me lord," I replied.

"I just like that man to appear in my court; he is so knowledgeable and easy going".

He went on to ask me, "What case do we have for tomorrow?"

"Oh, we have Lucien Genet v Sorie Pasarel", I replied.

"Oh that one", he said. This was a civil case involving debt. The plaintiff, Lucien Genet, was a French naturalised Sierra Leonean who was a prominent businessman. He owned a very big store, Lucien Genet and Son, between the junction of Westmoreland Street(Siaka Stevens Street) and Wilberforce Street. He was one of the first mayors of Freetown after Independence. There's no doubt that I gained much from such close interaction with such learned men.

Government ministers had so many privileges, for example, facilities for hire purchases from big stores like Kingsway, and P.Z (Patterson Zochonis). Sometimes they misused these privileges. A junior minister whose dad, a well-known senior minister was co-defendant in one such case. The defendant owed Lucien Genet over Le2,000.00, equivalent to £1,000. There was a court order for the defendant to pay a certain amount every month but he never did. Justice Harding had adjourned the case on several occasions because the man never paid anything. The judge was fed-up. When I mentioned that this was the one we had the next day, his reply was, "Oh that one! I'm going to lock him up for contempt if he doesn't start paying tomorrow". Next day the case was called up and the defendant had no lawyer to plead on his behalf. The plaintiff's lawyer said a few words and the judge said, "This case has been going on for a long time and I'm fed up of sitting on it. Have you brought any money to make your first payment?"

"No, me lord," the defendant replied. He was sweating at this stage; he knew something was going to happen. I knew as well. I felt sorry for him, and with some quick thinking I wrote a short note to the judge, pleading with him to give him one last chance. I stated on the note that he was my friend, and I did not want him to be disgraced by sending him to prison. Some would say this was disgraceful nepotism that interferred with the course of justice, and thus a step too far. At this stage, Justice Harding changed his mind and remarked,

"I wanted to send you down but God saved you." Did he mean me? He then warned the accused: "Next time you appear before me and you have not made any payment to this court I don't care two hoots, you will go down." These were his favourite words - "two hoots." I knew I could not save my friend the next time.

Previously we had dealt with a trade dispute involving two popular Lebanese businessmen in a trademark case for a popular mosquito coil. The plaintiff took the defendant to court for producing similar trademarks. A popular Freetown lawyer, Pa McCormack acted for the plaintiff, and the case went on for a while. After a short adjournment, Justice Harding called me to his chambers. "Mr Tucker", he said, "you see Lebanese, they like to bribe people to get what they want; never you take a penny from them or they are bound to tell others." He went on, "Don't mind that Yazbeck" (another popular Lebanese businessman in Freetown, the main Mercedes-Benz dealer in the country.) "He wants to buy my Benz; it's now a vintage car. Justice Harding was probably the only person in Freetown to have this old type of Benz, coloured black and always looking immaculate, as if he'd just bought it brand new. "He thinks I'm a fool," he said "he wants to put it in his showroom. If I sell that car to him he will send it to Germany and sell it for a fortune." With his cigar in his hand, he went on: "Mr Tucker, you know why I studied law?"

"No my lord," I replied. "You see me, I used to work at Cable & Wireless; someone insulted my mother when I was a young man causing me to vow to study law one day."

I promptly replied, "And you did it; today you are a top judge".

I'm ever so grateful to Justice Harding for all these little things he taught me. Whilst I was attached to work with him in court he had confidence in me. I got a gift of £50 from him when I was leaving for England - the equivalent of Le.100.00. in those days.

An experience I had whilst working in the law courts was what you will term, "from the sublime to the ridiculous". Appeal court session was on. W with me was my lifelong friend, Edmett Benjamin, who was attached to the magistrate's court office. We just went to look at these three great appeals court judges in action: Justices S.B Jones, who was then President of the Court of Appeal, Justice Forster and a Sri-Lankan Judge. Suddenly the "Black Maria", that is the prison van, arrived in the courtyard. Word reached everybody in the building that a very notorious prisoner was appearing in the Court of Appeal. Previously, he had been sentenced to death for a murder he committed in Kenema, a very nice district town in the Eastern Province. Soon the courtyard was full. It was 'Highway', a notorious gangster. Hhe was like the Kray twins of the East End of London. I used to hear the name, 'Highway,' but had never seen him before.

Suddenly Edmett said to me, "Look at him, they are coming." 'The prisoner was handcuffed to a tough warder and accompanied by four other warders.

"You know who that is?" Edmett said, "That's the 'Highway. In fact, he did not finish what he was saying to me and there was 'Highway' right in front of me. I was shaking with fear. He was tall and had bulging eyes, as if to cast a spell on me. He said to me,

"Brother please give me a cigarette." I went straight down to the courtyard and bought a large packet of Benson and Hedges, came up and gave it to him. He said, "God bless you, brother,"staring at me as if he was memorising my face. I thought I was going to defecate in my trousers! 'Highway' was then arraigned before the court with Mr. Riby-Williams, deputising for Dr. Marcus Jones as the defending lawyer. The legal arguments started, and Edmett, and I left the courtroom returning to our respective offices. By the time we came up again they were delivering their judgement to the court. It was sensational. 'Highway' won the appeal! A week later, this man came to see me in my office at the law courts. Hhe was always smartly dressed in those days, with 'Beatle' boots, tergal trousers, a long sleeved pullover, gold bracelet and gold chain. He was very fashionable, walking the streets of Freetown with all the latest designs. Those who knew him would point their fingers at him to show others, or wave to him. He took a likiing to me because of that packet of cigarettes I had bought for him. He always came to the law courts to say hello to me. He also got to know that I was an official of mighty Blackpool Football Club from the west end of Freetown. He was a very strong supporter of East End Lions from the east end of Freetown.

One day Mr. Woode said to me, "Tucker, I want you to accompany Mr. Reffell on trek." He could see that I didn't know what he meant, and laughed.

"You look confused," he said. "This will give you an opportunity to know the country.Listen, man, Circuit Court is coming up soon in Makeni, and one of your favourite Judges, O.B.R Tejan, is going to preside."

I said okay since I had never been to Makeni before; the nearest I had been was to Rokupr, the rice research station. It was when I lived with Mr. Victor George-Pratt, the Permanent Secretary of the Ministry of the Interior. We had had to cross the wide Mange River on the ferry I used to hear so much about and spent the day at the research station.

We set off for Makeni the following week with a senior driver, Ade Cole, driving the official Land Rover. I took my Phillips transistor radio with me so that I could listen to

Radio Brazzaville at 5.45 p.m. It was my favourite radio station outside Sierra Leone. The Phillips transistor radio had been introduced by a former Minister of Information, the Honourable John Nelson–Williams. Prior to that, most ordinary households had a radio, a small box supplied by the former Post and Telecommunications Department as part of a rediffusion service. The only stations we could listen to were the British Broadcasting Corporation (BBC) overseas service, and the Sierra Leone Broadcasting Service (SLBS). We used to call it "Congosa Box". We had no alternative unless, of course, you were an aristocrat, and could afford to obtain a Radiogram, a better system that enabled you to receive many stations around the world.

Ade Cole drove brilliantly, we left Freetown around 11.00 a.m. and arrived safely in Makeni a few hours later. Moses Reffell and Egbert Thomas, my colleagues, had been there before, so they had already negotiated with a Mrs. Allen of Mabanta Road for our accommodation. She seemed a very kind lady and had a son who happened to be my friend, and a student at the University of Sierra Leone. When Mrs. Allen realised my relationship with David, she made me feel more at home, thereby once again gaining an advantage from 'who knows me.' We briefed a lawyer , Bunting Thompson, Counsel representing some defendants in a manslaughter case. Mrs. Allen prepared a lovely dinner for us on our arrival: rice with a very delicious cassava leaves sauce, which is my favourite.

I fell in love with Makeni straight away. I woke up in the morning and heard women pounding and dying gara clothing materials, using the 'tie dye' process. I liked the smell of the special dye made from special plants.

I came in contact with very friendly people. One day after the court session, we decided to tour the area. We started off by visiting a town called Tekor, where the government agriculturist resided in one of the beautiful government quarters. On our way home, we drove along Tekor Road and I noticed a photographer's shop. I asked the driver to give me ten minutes to go and buy a film for my camera. To my surprise, when I approached the owner of the shop, I discovered my long-lost classmate from Murray Town Primary School, David King Taylor, now a big time photographer in Makeni! This did not surprise me because since we were in class together he used to have an old type box Kodak camera, taking pictures and charging for them, not knowing that he would later make a career and living out of it. We were so happy to be reunited after over fifteenyears. "Where are you putting up?" he asked.

"Mabanta Road," I replied, "with a Mrs. Allen."

Most people knew Mrs. Allen. I then gave him my work schedule for the following day which ended at 4 p.m. He stopped by after our session ended, and we spent a good time together. We did this regularly until we left for Freetown.

The whole court session proved most educational, with lots of interesting cases. Most of these were adjourned until the next session. The trip was also a pleasant experience as it gave me the opportunity to meet some nice people in beautiful Makeni. I'm ever so grateful for my experience with the justices, and for the invaluable lessons I learnt so early in my working career about application and hard work that would serve me in good stead in my new life overseas.

Law Courts building, central Freetown – my former workplace

Colleagues in the Master's office, after an Assize church service at St George's Cathedral in 1970. At the back (L-R)- Mr Horton, Mr Bright, Miss Tarawallie, Mr Njie, Mr Higgson, the librarian. From (L-R) Mr Spaine and Sigismond.

Chapter 8

Our "resource curse"

In 2009, prospectors discovered oil in Sierra Leone, the latest in the numerous natural resources with which our tiny country has been blessed. At the very least, having Gold, Bauxite, Iron Ore, Platinum, Diamonds and Rutile should have been a blessing and not the curse it has turned out to be for our people. Alas, I fear that this latest discovery holds no prospect of greater prosperity, or real wealth for the population. Indeed, I agree with the expert view that without prompt action to increase transparency, the people of Sierra Leone will only continue under the burden of the "resource curse," steeped in abject poverty and probably under renewed threat of civil conflict. In recent decades, few countries have experienced the tragedy and devastation of our brutal civil war, fuelled mainly by an illicit trade in diamonds.

For years, our leaders have mismanaged revenue generated from natural resources through endemic greed, and embraced wholeheartedly the corruption arising from nepotism or a patronage system. Rather than directing resources toward rebuilding the state, and improving the lives of ordinary citizens, a handful of political elites have individually misappropriated state resources accumulated from diamonds, minerals, and no doubt oil in the future. Without an effective structure of accountability, this latest discovery is bound to return the country to conflict, and trigger a reversal of hard-won democratic gains since the end of the war.

The evils in our society are that of corruption and nepotism, selfishness, tribalism and greed. We have so much wealth in Sierra Leone that if administered fairly, everyone would have a piece of the cake. The words of the late Pastor Edward Edwards who mused all those years ago that, "We Africans are walking on top of gold, yet we are so poor," are as true now as then. We are quick to take our begging bowls to the west to feed our hungry, and to look after our sick. I am so infuriated when I see children here on British television collecting money for the dying, and starving in Africa, when it was African leaders and the irresponsible politicians of the 60s and 70s who ripped off their countries' wealth by virtue of their political positions. In my opinion, politicians are mainly responsible for laundering millions of pounds to Swiss banks and other overseas financial institutions. Some of these rogues, without any regard for the suffering masses, can afford to send their children, and relatives to the West for education. They send their wives and girlfriends to the West on expensive shopping sprees and purchase luxury housing, and the poor people don't have a clue what their so-called representatives are doing. Yet due to such handicaps like tribalism and illiteracy, these same masses are prepared to die for their leaders by harassing, or killing opponents, burning houses and waving fists and machetes in the air. Sometimes I see them on television and I say to myself: the lack of education is a dangerous thing; if only these people could understand how they are making life hell for themselves, they won't be doing all these stupid things.

Our country was a 'free for all' state. With little or no immigration control and with bribery and corruption amongst officials, it was easy for these strangers to come and stay anywhere in the country. The main destination for some of these foreigners was Kono, the land of diamonds. Things came to a head at the departure from office of Sir Maurice Dorman who had been our last Governor, and first Governor- General at Independence. During a parliamentary debate M.Ps spoke on Sir Maurice's departure: The Minister of Finance, Mr M. S. Mustapha talked favourably of the way Sir Maurice helped put the country's case in financial talks. The atmosphere changed abruptly as Messrs J Barthes-Wilson, I. T. A. Wallace-Johnson and T. S. Mbriwa spoke. Mr Barthes-Wilson stated that he only had a good relationship with Fort Thornton after the National Front. *"Sir Maurice contributed to the economic starvation of the country by driving Guineans away,"* Mr Wallace-Johnson said, amid booing by some M.Ps. Mr T S Mbriwa stated that to say that he was sorry for the departure of Sir Maurice would be hypocritical. He said that in fact,, he was very happy to see him go. He ended by saying that when Sir Maurice went to Kono he said, *"Guineans go away from our country,"* and now Sierra Leoneans say *"Sir Maurice go away from our country."* You can't help some people!

Apparently, Sir Maurice's edict turned into the greatest chagrin of some Members of Parliament. In addition to this mass extradition, the government passed a bill whereby indigenous Sierra Leoneans were required to have a government permit in order to settle within Sierra Leone Selection Trust areas. To qualify for a permit an individual had to have a recognised job to do in the area. Needless to say, this was most unacceptable, and led to the second case quoted below.

This failure in policy has come back to bite us. Today, we hear that the main cause of the eleven years rebel war was for control of the illegal diamond trade, financed mainly for self-gain. Witness the Charles Taylor trial, and there can be no doubt that the diamond mines and the need to bring in South Africans to defend those mines some of whom have stayed on to secure the right to continue mining, had a part to play during the civil war.

I recall two classic diamond cases of bribery and corruption that involved foreigners. Case number one occurred around 1964 in the state versus Koulubaley, a Gambian national and diamond dealer living in Kono. He was arrested, tried and as a result ordered to leave the country. The police officer, responsible for executing the deportation order, Inspector Cyril Grant, was well known in the city. On their way to board the boat, Koulubaley spotted an iron bar, grabbed it, and hit the officer on the head repeatedly, killing him on the spot. He was charged with murder. The charge was reduced to manslaughter, and he was sent to prison for ten years. Again bribery and corruption was highlighted in this case. It was alleged in his defence that after the police officer received money from him, he betrayed Koulubaley, and was at the forefront of his deportation.

The other classic diamond case in Freetown was referred to as, "The Kono Diamond Permit Case" around 1969-970, involving over twenty printing officials. In the latter part of Sir Albert Margai's tenure as Prime Minister, the government decided that every non-Sierra Leonean who wanted to enter Kono must have a government permit because Kono was becoming overcrowded with foreigners. There also became a popular song titled, 'All Den Maraka for Go,. As a result, the 'Kono Permit' was a very welcome government decision at the time.

A leading Lebanese businessman, Shammel, and twenty or more printing officials, were caught in the act. They were accused of printing a substantial number of permits, above the government quotas issued for a particular period. This gang allegedly sold these extra permits for huge sums of money. Charges were made and they were brought to the magistrate courts in Freetown. One of Freetown's leading lawyers, Cyrus Rogers-Wright, represented Shammel. The case was committed to the Supreme Court and all the depositions and evidence was brought up to our office. Theaccused were supposed to be under lock and key. One of our working colleagues was put in charge of the case files and other documents tendered in the magistrate court. That was a big mistake. Such a sensitive case needed a strong and honest character to be in charge of these files and depositions. More honest clerks like Thomas Bright, Egbert Thomas, Moses Reffell, Alex Kamara and I were busy with the treason trials.   We all knew that it was just a matter of time before this fellow was caught in his hanky-panky and thirst for money in that office. On reflection, I wish we had reported our concerns in a timely manner.

This trial was sensational. With defence lawyers like Cyrus Rogers-Wright, it did not last long, and it was not surprising that for lack of evidence he got an acquittal for all his clients, including Shammel. My dishonest colleague was subsequently charged with Perverting the Course of Justice.

We were all desperate in those days to have more money because wages were low, but as the saying goes, 'money is the root of all evil'. There is a limit to which one can go. If one tries to live beyond his means, then working in a place like the law courts can lead you astray due to the many temptations. There were good and generous lawyers around who would appreciate the work the clerks did for them. Sometimes they would call you to their chambers and give you tips as a show of appreciation. Most times we had honest ways of earning extra money, for instance, preparing affidavits for clients whose lawyers required such documents for their cases. My colleagues and I would prepare these affidavits for clients before passing them to a Commissioner of Oaths, most times to Mr Ralph Woode, for the clients to swear an oath with the bible or the Koran. An affidavit in those days would cost £1, which was Le 2.00. Our team consisted of Alex Kamara, I.B.K.(real name I.B.Kamara) the bailiff, and Mr Ralph Woode Senior Registrar and Commissioner of Oaths. The latter also charged clients £1 for taking the oath. I.B.K gave us constant referrals to clients who required affidavit declaration.

We are now left with the diamond mines being under the control of South Africans at Koidu, on the one hand, and Israelis of the Octea Diamond mining group in northern Kono on the other. We have thus come a long way from 1972 when Diminco African Mine found the third largest rough diamond (968.80 carats) at the Diminco mine, cut it into 17 stones, six of which are now set in the Star of Sierra Leone Brooch.

Chapter 9

The Early Treason Trials

Almost thirty- eight years ago on 19th July 1975, a sad chapter was written in the political history of Sierra Leone when Dr. Mohamed Sorie Forna, one of Sierra Leone's most brilliant politicians, together with Lieutenant Habib Lansana Kamara, Ibrahim Bash Taqi, Brigadier David Lansana, and Paramount Chief Bai Makarie N'silk, were hangedat the notorious Pademba Road Prison in Freetown. Displaying the bodies for about an hour outside the prison walls, sent shock waves throughout Sierra Leone, and even beyond.

Siaka Stevens's popularity as leader of the All People's Congress and Prime Minister of Sierra Leone started to erode in 1971 when his government executed Brigadier John Bangura - the man who literally handed over power to him in 1968 - together with Jawara and Kolugbonda. The three were the first high-ranking officers to be executed in Sierra Leone after independence in 1961. Sources very close to prison authorities then have it that Brigadier John Bangura wept at the eleventh hour to his execution - finding it hard to believe that Siaka Stevens, the man he had installed in office, had rejected his plea for mercy. It was also revealed that Bangura never faced the gallows: he was beaten to death when he refused to make his last walk to the gallows. What a terrible way to end, for a decorated officer held in such high esteem!

The marathon trial of Mohamed Sorie Forna (Siaka Stevens' former Minister of Finance) and fourteen others, riveted the nation. And the eventual execution of Dr. Forna and Ibrahim Taqi (former Information Minister), two distinguished Sierra Leoneans who played a pivotal role in the All People's Congress election victory in 1967 - was not only a burden of grief to family and loved ones, but a terrible loss to the entire nation. It was a national act of terror that had immediate and far-reaching repercussions. The executions alienated the support of many northerners, especially at Tonkolili (an APC political stronghold during the 1967 General Election) and increased the level of popular discontent against Siaka Stevens.

About a year before the treason trial of David Lansana began in the Supreme Court, the first task was to re-swear Cyril Rogers-Wright to the Bar. The main aim for him getting back to the bar, I later found out, was for him to become the first prosecuting counsel working for the Crown Law Office. There were prominent lawyers like Teddy Wyndham, Mr Adophy, St. Barnard (a West Indian Lawyer), all of whom had been in the judiciary for long and had a wealth of experience. That notwithstanding, Cyril Rogers-Wright was appointed Chief Prosecutor. We were first of all going to deal with all the 1967 election petitions that were filed against all the members of Parliament who gained their seats unopposed. This was another example of corrupt practices in our electoral system in which intimidation featured prominently. Ruling party supporters sometimes severely beat up opponents, even prominent people who wanted to contest a seat, so that they could not meet registration deadlines. Therefore, the members of the ruling party were invariably declared unopposed. Some of these so-called unopposed members lost their seats in Parliament. Despite his tricks, Cyril

Rogers-Wright , was a brilliant lawyer. In court, he cleverly cited relevant portions of the electoral rule clauses which were mainly contained in Rule 19. "Rule 19" thus became a prominent household expression in the country. This was a political victory for Cyril, seen by some as some kind of vendetta. Personally he was quite opposed to the rampant "unopposed" results in elections.

Shortly after the election cases, the treason trial of David Lansana and 14 others was to begin. They were all detained in Pademba Road Prison. There were rumours that on account of their wealth, some of the accused were going to be represented by some of the best English barristers.. In fact, there was a widespread rumour that Dingle Foot QC, a prominent London barrister, would come, but he never did. Instead, three other barristers came from London. They were Cook, Murray and De Silva. Other local lawyers represented some other accused. Amongst the accused was Berthan Macaulay QC who was Attorney General during the Albert Margai Government. Berthan Macaulay defended himself throughout the trial. He was brilliant, and I liked him very much.

The first problem we had when the trial started was the swearing in of the jurors. This was an enormous task. In the normal way the accused objected to several candidates, until finally we got the twelve. Next step was the task of reading the charges to all fourteen of them, one by one. My colleague Alex Kamara did this. When that was completed, amendments were made to the indictments as necessary. The trial on the whole was very costly, in terms of barristers' pay both local and foreign. Also, lunch was provided for all staff and Jurors, which made me very happy. As a poor clerk, I had free lunch for the duration. The trial gave me the opportunity to see brilliant lawyers at their best. My boss, Chief Justice C.O.E Cole, was ushered into court by "Pa" During after taking one or two shots of hard liquor. It seemed that the alcohol increased his knowledge of law. I am sure the British barristers thought they were going to have an easy walk over because they were in Africa or Sierra Leone for that matter. I guess they quickly realised that a brilliant African lawyer was a force to be reckoned with after all. Cyril Rogers-Wright, the chief Crown Prosecutor and Berthan Macaulay were marvellous to watch, but I believe that Cyrus-Rogers-Wright surpassed his father in court.

The trial lasted for almost a year, and ended with the death penalty being passed on David Lansana. The whole episode proved a terrible experience for me. That was the first time I had the opportunity to witness such a solemn moment when the jury returned their verdict of Guilty of treason on David Lansana. The judge went to his chambers and re-appeared, this time in a black robe. "Pa During" placed the black cloth on top of his wig in order to pronounce the death sentence. I found it both scary, and sorrowful, and I wept inside as they took him down; he had twenty-onedays to launch an appeal.

For a while the Supreme Court had a break, and I went back to the civil jurisdiction and continued to work with my favourite judges, Justice Donald Macaulay and Justice Roland Harding. I particularly liked those two Judges because they taught me a lot, and I felt protected when I was with either of them. Meanwhile, preparations were being made for the trial of Brigadier Juxon-Smith and Brigadier John Bangura.

Their trial followed the same pattern as that of David Lansana, with Justice C.O.E Cole, Alex Kamara clerk of court, and me as his assistant. By this time I had much experience from the first treason trial. I now understood all the proceedings that followed. The three lawyers that came from London had already left and it was all local barristers - GeorgeGelaga-King and Doe Smith. No one represented Juxon-Smith, as he was trying to defend himself. At this stage, I felt sorry for the man, as I saw the strain in his face. I went home and told his wife to try and see if they could get someone to represent him, and Cyrus Rogers-Wright agreed to so act. This was nearly half way through the trial. Again the leading prosecuting council was Cyril Rogers-Wright, father of Cyrus Roger-Wright. It was exciting to see father and son in court exchanging legal arguments, but the father was no match for the son, which was a well known fact within the legal circles in Sierra Leone at the time.

I got to know Juxon-Smith properly in court, although I used to see him regularly when he was at Murray Town Barracks. But he knew me well in court because I was always with the family and most times I was his main means of communication between himself, and his wife. Whilst he was in court, I was also privileged to meet his mother, a Mende lady who was from the Eastern Province. Not quite sure whether she was from Kailahun or Pujehun. She came to town regularly to spend time with her daughter-in-law, Miss Laddie, her daughter Madiana Neneh and grandchildren Solomon and Andrew. There is a general opinion among Sierra Leoneans that Juxon-Smith should have remained in power for at least another four to five years to bring that country up to standard and discipline. I'm sure those who remember him from the short period he was in power all share this view. However, for the vicious lies and propaganda carried against him by Siaka Stevens and his A.P.C machinery craving for power, others hold the view that he was arrogant, and also wanted to declare the country a Republic and become the first president. No doubt, political commentators and students of history will pass judgement on that.

─────── **Chapter 10** ───────

The era of Commissions of Inquiry

Sierra Leone is a beautiful country despite those bandits and hooligans who, tried so desperately to destroy it during the rebel war. A solid, sound, and unified government was left for us by Sir Milton Margai, our pioneer of Independence in 1961. Under him everything was fine; small, and soft spoken as he was, he tolerated no nonsense from anyone.

Sir Milton Margai was believed to be grooming Dr. John Karefa-Smart to succeed him as Prime Minister. He was such an able politician, the kind of no-nonsense man who may well have proved to be an effective prime minister. There could have been a unified government in our country devoid of the menace of tribalism. However, instead, Sir Milton's wishes were thwarted when Albert Margai was recalled to join, and lead the S.L.P.P immediately after his death, and Albert became Prime Minister.

This marked the beginning of a new style of politics in Sierra Leone, dominated by tribalism, nepotism and corruption. People can notice one dominant tribe flourishing. Bad political decision-making through the leadership was in fact what brought about Albert Margai's downfall in the 1967 general election. His decision not to give L.A.M Brewah and Kai-Samba the S.L.P.P symbol for the election, leading them to stand as independent candidates, and the ensuing chaos, was a contributory factor to his downfall.

Corruption during his reign was rife. Rice, the staple food in the country, was so easy to get, and was cheap everywhere. Even the poor could afford to buy rice by the bag, or by the cupful according to their needs. However, his government decided to set up a rice co-operation, and soon a lot of people started to profit by doing illegal business with rice coupons.

In a shiort time, the country began to experience scarcity of rice. Ministers' wives, and girlfriends, senior civil servants, soldiers' wives and some other people with influence, including some with certain religious affiliations, started hoarding rice, and selling at exorbitant prices on the black market. Very soon, the ordinary people in Sierra Leone were beginning to suffer, barely able to get a cup of rice. Many people thought that the events that followed amounted to inexcusable disgrace for government. Immediately after the 1967 chaos, there were commissions of enquiry. The two most famous commissions were the Justice Forster Commission of Enquiry and the Justice Percy Davies Commission of Enquiry. One of the ministries targeted was the Ministry of Trade, and Industry which was responsible for the Rice Corporation, and the Sierra Leone Produce Marketing Board (S.L.P.M.B). Some of the revelations were scandalous. For example, when asked to give account of missing tonnes of bags of rice, officials came up with frivolous excuses including: "Rats ate them," or "Hundreds of bags rotted." It was just unbelievable. But as usual, nothing came of these probes. They were merely a waste of resources, and the time these commissioners spent looking into them and writing their reports. People found guilty were not given the maximum punishments for their malpractices, corruption and greed. As the Sierra Leoneans say, "Nar buff case," meaning, "Nothing will come out it". This is one of the problems in Sierra Leone.

People are not made to respect the rule of law which is very important for a society to function effectively. In our society, some people will do things they know are wrong, and in the end somebody in high places will lobby for them to get away with their wrong doings.

Another institution where rampant corruption existed was the Ministry of Education. In those days, the country had so many Commonwealth bursaries and scholarships, some of which went to the wrong hands. Most times deserving students were bypassed. The Russian Government offered scholarships to deserving Sierra Leoneans, but these were manipulated by the Ministry of Education. For example, my friend Edward Tomaku applied and fortunately he got the scholarship to go, and study science at a Russian University. It was confirmed, and everything was set. My mother, Sissy, was a good friend of Tomaku's mum whom we called Mama Tomaku. A day was set for a send-off party. I will never forget that day because my mother helped Mama Tomaku to prepare food. She ground bBlack-eyed beans to make what we call in Sierra Leone "Binch Akara" a kind of fritter. The celebrations went on as planned and everything was fine. However, a week later, when Tomaku went to the Ministry to check on some documentation, he found a line across his name on the notice board replaced by another name. He had suffered a brutal shock, and came home almost in tears. These were the sorts of things that went on in my country. Undaunted, Tomaku went on to apply at Njala University to study Science. Three years later he graduated with a BSc. degree and that's what I called a determined guy. I believe that if he had gone to Russia, he would have come home with a doctorate. He continued to teach at

Roosevelt Secondary School for Girls, but remained a broken man from what they did to him at the Ministry. One morning he complained of a stomachache, and said he was going to Connaught Hospital. Sadly, on arrival, he suddenly collapsed, and passed away: a young man with so much to offer to our country, brought down by the prevailing corrupt, and tribalistic practices.

In 1990, I went to Freetown, after almost twenty years away, to attend my younger brother Emmanuel Lati King's wedding. Of course, everything I saw in the country disappointed me, especially the way my friend 'Major General Doctor' Momoh was running (some might say 'ruining') the country. It saddened me to see the parade of Pajeros, Mercedes Benzes and other fancy vehicles, against a background of abject poverty in the country. All one heard people saying was, "This man" or "That man is a tycoon", and yet there was hardly any electricity. Every corner I turned, I heard the continuous hum of generators. I learnt that just two weeks before my arrival in Freetown, five people from the same family died in a house, near Jokie Bridge in Freetown. They had arrived on holiday from England, and had kept their generator running inside the house for fear of thieves. Tragically, the generator's carbon monoxide fumes suffocated them, and they all perished. What a way to die!

Before I left Sierra Leone in 1971, it was already becoming so corrupt that life was becoming a matter of survival of the fittest. For every single official transaction you had to be prepared to bribe an official. It was done on such a scale that the phrase "Put for me" became the national anthem, that is to say; you had to give money to an official before he or she would perform their duty. Sometimes you would be told that the person who was supposed to sign a document for you needed "kola", meaning some money as bribery. It is no wonder that somebody could have a new job and ,ithin a very short time, you would hear that he or she was building two or three houses somewhere. Another phenomenon that came out in some of commissions of enquiry was that of non-existing staff or ghost workers whose names appeared on pay-rolls whilst someone else received their salaries. Some senior officials would report for work in the morning, and in no time would leave to go on personal errands. These were some of the practices that Brigadier Juxon-Smith was determined to eradicate from our society; unfortunately he was not given the chance. I remember that one of the methods he used was to make impromptu visits to various government offices to find out who arrived late, or who was absent. He would be there as they were opening the front door. Who dare not be in his office on time, or not stay there all day?

Under subsequent rulers, things did not improve. Government officials became very distrustful of each other, as you never knew who was a secret informant for the government in power. If you mistakenly said the 'wrong' word you would be reported, and stood a good chance of losing your job as a result. An example of this occurredin 1990, when I visited the country. I happened to visit a friend who was Assistant Secretary, Ministry of Development, in the six-story Yui Building at Brookfields. As usual, there was no electricity and the lifts were not working. I had to walk upstairs, and I think I was going to the 4th floor. For every floor I passed through, messengers who were supposed to accompany, or direct visitors had their small trays selling cola nuts, cigarettes and tobacco. I said to myself:, this is disgusting. I finally located my friend, and the first thing I asked her was, "Why are those messengers selling in front of the place?" She replied, "You've not seen anything yet; this is a common thing. If you speak or take action, you will be reported to a minister, so we just shut our mouth." With all this going on in my country, I concluded that Sierra Leone was like a time bomb waiting to explode.

Sir Milton Margai hosting HM The Queen

Dr John Karefa Smart

━━━━━━━━ **Chapter 11** ━━━━━━━━

Major John Bangura Signing his own death warrant

Whilst in America, Siaka Stevens negotiated with Bangura to leave his post and help train his political thugs and mercenaries in neighbouring Guinea to come and overthrow the then military leader of Sierra Leone, Andrew Juxon-Smith. Siaka Stevens then believed he was the winner of the 1967 election, and that he had been robbed of victory, by the 1967 coup, led by Brigadier David Lansana, Police Commissioner Leigh, and others. In reality he was not, because the election was neck and neck, and independent candidates were going to decide the outright winners - candidates like Kutubu Kai-Samba, and a practising Lawyer, L.A.M Brewah. Anyway, this was not to be as Siaka Stevens was installed in power by John Bangura after a brief spell in power of a Military Government called the National Reformation Council (NRC). It came to power as a result of the uncertainties that followed the1967 general elections.

John Bangura was head of this military government for about six months, after which he decided to hand over power to Siaka Stevens to head a civilian national unity government. This was the beginning of his downfall. The first thing Stevens did was to form an alliance with Sekou Toure, the first President of Guinea. This alliance enabled them to protect each other in case of any security threat to their rule: "You scratch my back and I'll scratch yours". Very soon, we started seeing Guinean soldiers all over Freetown, with guns and machetes strapped to their hips.

Others were posted at State House, and at the private residence of Stevens at King Harman Road in Brookfields. This move was solely for to protect himself since he did not have much faith and trust in our soldiers.

Whilst Siaka Stevens was now Prime Minister, Bangura became Brigadier and head of the army. It is common for African soldiers to promote themselves or be promoted to ranks which are questionable. Another example was a soldier who was a Lieutenant when they seized power from General Momoh, and who ended up being a Brigadier after he seized power from his fellow soldier. What a mockery!

Anyway, coming back to Brigadier Bangura: putting Siaka Stevens in power, he thought he had done a great job. Indeed it was a great job. He was the most powerful man in the country at that time; this, I think, went to his head. His good friend was the lawyer Cyrus Rogers-Wright, who was also my friend. Cyrus lived not too far from me at Aberdeen Ferry Road.

One day I was visiting Cyrus when Bangura also came to visit. At that moment I had some beautiful foreign stamps which I was collecting, and was showing them to Cyrus. Bangura, seeing these said to me, "Can I buy them from you? I collect stamps myself." He probably thought because he was wearing his full uniform with all his glittering medals, I would be intimidated, and agree to his proposal. I simply declined his offer. Cyrus had heard him and winked to tell me to refuse this offer.

I once remember Bangura returning from America with a big American car which he used to drive around town. It was a sky blue Chevrolet. One problem about these foreign cars being imported was the question of getting spare parts to repair them when something went wrong. He was lucky he got someone who had knowledge of these cars and he was lucky the man he had to repair this monster car was a specialist in these cars. He was in charge of the American Embassy vehicle maintenance department. He He lived next door to us in Byrne Lane, Aberdeen Ferry Road, was called Harold "Dombolo" and wasa brilliant motor mechanic.

After repairing Bangura's car quite perfectly and returning it to good running order, you would never guess what happened next. We had a farewell party for "Dombolo" in his house. He was going to England the next day. Two weeks later he was back in town, now as lieutenant "Harold Dombolo" which I'm sure was a reward for repairing that monster car. In addition to becoming a lieutenant, he was placed in charge of the transport maintenance section at Juba Barracks. Everybody around doubted that he did come to England to be commissioned because the man had no prior military training. You see the extent of corruption in my country!

The Army was very powerful during the time of Bangura. They held the balance of power, and just a little blunder was enough to topple the civilian government. Soldiers often intimidated civilians. Our man Harold was one of them. He had an open American jeep, with a Guinean called Mahmudu as his driver. Harold looked very smart in his uniform and he would sometimes put his feet up on the dashboard of the jeep, whilst Mahmudu drove him everywhere. Everyone at Byrne Lane was scared of him; he now drank and socialised with the big shots in town. As First Lieutenant, he now considered himself an aristocrat.

One Saturday, my football team 'Mighty Blackpool' had a match, so I came home late that day. Usually on Saturday nights when I had nowhere to go, I would hang out at the Texaco filling station, situated at the junction of Wilkinson Road and Aberdeen Ferry Road. By 10 p.m. I left for home and just as I was approaching Byrne Lane, I had this loud swearing. Someone was insulting Harold's mother with the vilest of words. In Sierra Leone, to swear at someone and his mother would immediately provoke a big fight. As I got closer, the swearing was getting more vulgar. I then realised that it was my friend Alex Cotey who was swearing at Harold.

"What's wrong?" I asked him.

"Na dis basta pekin," (this bastard) who hit me very hard on the face simply because he was smoking, and I asked him to light my cigarette for me since I was not carrying a match or lighter."

Harold considered it an audacity on my friend's part to ask him to light his cigarette. Alex was about nineteenyears old, completing his "A" levels at the Albert Academy. You can imagine what it felt like to be hit on the face by a huge man. I felt sorry for that poor lad that night, as his face was already swollen.

Anyway, I calmed him down because he wanted to stab Harold with a broken bottle, and that could have been fatal. I took him to his house just about 400 yards from the incident. On my return, Harold approached me and asked, "Humble, is that your friend?" When I replied that he was indeed my friend, he further asked, "Who is he?" I then said.

"He's Magistrate Cotey's son. I deliberately used the word Magistrate so that Harold would know whose son he was messing with – indirectly telling him that he could be in big trouble if he was not careful.

The next day, Sunday, Harold went to Juba Barracks, got three soldiers, went to arrest Alex inside his house. This should have put Harold in more trouble because it was a wrongful arrest without a warrant. He and his assistants threw my friend inside the Land Rover and took him to Juba Barracks, locked him up in the Guard Room, and ordered him to scrub the floor of the toilet. I was staying next door to Harold. When he came back, I was ironing my clothes when I heard his voice calling me, "Humble! Humble"! I replied "yes". He then went on, "Your friend, Alex - I have taught him a lesson; he thinks he is cheeky." Up to that moment I never knew what he had done to Alex. A few minutes later Mrs. Cotey's driver, Allieu, came to tell me that Alex's mum whom he called "Missis" wanted to see me. "What for"? I asked. Allieu replied that a soldier and his assistants came to the house, gave Alex a good beating, and took him away. I went to the house to meet Mrs. Cotey, then a Matron at Fourah Bay College, University of Sierra Leone. She explained to me what Allieu had told me earlier. "He is your friend.",she said. "Please go and find out where he took him.Allieu will take you in the car." It was a white Peugeot. I agreed and told Allieu to take me to Murray Town Barracks. All the guards on duty knew me. I explained to them what happened, and they advised me to go to Juba barracks, Harold's base.

We drove to Juba and met the guards on duty playing a game of draughts. As soon as they saw me, one of them asked, "Humble what have you come to do here this Sunday morning?" I explained to them what had happened to my friend, with Allieu standing by me. They all spoke together: "Humble, we are tired with this man "Dombolo". Ever since they brought him here as Lieutenant, we have been seeing hell in this place.Your friend is inside the guard house, he brought him here this morning". I heard Alex scrubbing the floor, and I shouted "Alex!"

"Yes", he replied.

"What are you doing there?" I asked.

"That bastard, with other soldiers, went and arrested me in the house this morning, and brought me to this place," Alex replied.

Allieu the driver drove me home and I told his Mum that I found him.

"Where did he take him?" she asked.

"He took him to Juba barracks", I replied.

She then asked Allieu to drive her to Banja, referring to Sir Banja Tejan-sie, the Governor-General of Sierra Leone at that time, who was her cousin. On the night of the altercation, I had tried to give a hint to "Dombolo" that he was treading on dangerous ground, but he was not smart enough to take the hint. Mrs. Cotey explained to Sir Banja what had happened and he just picked up the phone and called Brigadier Bangura. At around 2 p.m. Alex was released and sent home, on the instructions of the force commander, John Bangura. Allieu, the driver, came around and told me Alex was home. Meanwhile "Dombolo's" plan was to go and bring him home at 6 p.m. At about 5.30 p.m he saw me ironing from his compound and shouted, "Humble!"

"Yes," I replied.

"I am going for your friend, will you accompany me? I've taught him a bit of a lesson."

I replied that I would not be able to accompany him. To his surprise, when he went to Juba Barracks, he found out that Alex had been released since 1p.m on the instructions of the Force Commander, John Bangura.

What happened next? When "Dombolo" came home, he told his wife, and his neighbour friends that it was I who reported the matter to the Force Commander by phone, and that the fFrce Commander had scolded him. I became a hated person amongst his drinking friends. They were saying amongst themselves that I was a dangerous person politically because some of my friends who came to visit me were lawyers. They were referring, in particular, to Arnold Gooding, a barrister, who was with me most times because he loved playing table tennis. I was also friendly with Lawyer Cyrus Rogers-Wright, and my ministerfriend,

S.B Marah. With these people around me, they concluded that I had some political influence.

The next morning around 5 a.m., "Dombolo"'s wife was in her compound, quite naked, holding a glass of water, and pouring water on the ground, swearing. I saw her because I always woke up at this time to have my bath under the tap that was in the yard. She didn't see me. She was swearing in our local Krio language: "Ah wake dis morning, ah no eat pepeh or sol; Humble wan for take brade na me man e mot. God, nor make e able for do dis." That is to say, "I woke up this morning with an empty stomach, calling on God to intervene on our behalf; Humble wants to deprive us of our livelihood by putting my husband in trouble, and out of a job. God, do not let him succeed." I looked at the woman and felt sorry for her, with her very big naked butt and funny shape. I wanted to go, and call my mother to come and see because she was living a few hundred yards from us. On second thought, I decided not to do this, knowing how my hot-tempered mother would react. I later told her what had happened. Mrs. "Dombolo"'s group of friends, and my mother's own friends never spoke to each other again.

A few months after the "Dombolo" and Cotey incident, you would not believe what happened! Siaka Stevens was still Prime Minister and John Bangura was Force Commander. At that time John Bangura was regarded as the most powerful man in Sierra Leone and I think he realised that people were saying that if Siaka Stevens made one false step, he would topple him from power; as if they knew that was going to happen. To my surprise Harold "Dombolo" disappeared from his house for three days. You will not believe this. His wife was getting worried and approached me for the first time after swearing me few months earlier.

"Do ya Humble, you see Harold? Ah nor see am now for three days." That is to say, "Please, Humble, do you know the whereabouts of Harold? I have not seen him for three days."

I was tempted to use the "F" word, telling her to get out of my face. Instead, I simply said in Krio:

"Ah nor know," meaning, "I don't know," and went off.

Three days later, there was pandemonium in Freetown; there was talk of an attempted coup against Siaka Stevens. The main area of action was around State House, located in the centre of town. Guinean soldiers with guns and machetes, and Sierra Leonean soldiers were guarding State House, with bullets flying all over. Some of the bullets were hitting the Law Court Building, with courts in session. I was in Supreme Court number 1 with Justice Singer-Betts. I just read out the indictments against the accused. The situation was getting worse outside; people were fleeing from stray bullets, and for their lives. They were even running away from the courts. Then Justice Betts asked me, "Mr. Tucker, what's happening?" I replied that there was talk of a coup attempt. The first thing I did was to secure the case file, and the next was to help Justice Betts take cover underneath his desk. He was a very big man. Anyway, I eventually managed to lead him to his chambers. We were both breathing heavily, and quite exhausted. It was a 30-minutes chaos, with everybody trying to take cover. I went to lock up my case file in the safe because if it was lost, that would have been the end of that particular criminal case. Everybody was packing up to go home. The streets were in chaos, everybody running for cover, trying to get home. You were extremely lucky if you got a taxi or 'poda poda' (local mini-bus transportation) going towards your direction. There were soldiers in open trucks shooting at random intothe air. Guinean jets were flying over Freetown. It was frightening. As for me, I feared the Guinean soldiers more than our own soldiers. I finally made the decision to leave the Law Courts building and head for home. By that time the building was deserted. I said to myself: Do or die, I am heading home. I held my head, walking very fast, passing Kroo Town Road, and approaching King Tom Bridge. Suddenly I heard someone shout my name, "Humble, Humble."

"Yes," I replied and turned around. Luckily, it was Idrissa, a taxi driver friend who lived near us.

"Are you going home?"he asked.

"Yes," I replied.

"Come on, let me take you home," he said.

"Thank God, somebody up there sent you to save me," I said. I went home safely, with Guinean jets still flying all over the place.

Still Lieutenant "Dombolo" was nowhere to be seen; wife and children were crying. Next thing, we spotted him coming from the Collegiate School end towards

Byrne Lane, dressed as if he was from jungle warfare - long military khaki trousers, a short sleeved vest and the cartridge belt full of cartridges around his neck, and carrying a gun. He was amongst the coup-plotters. They used him, because of his mechanical skills, to break into the ammunition depot at Cockerill, leading towards Lumley Village. At that time, he did not know that the coup had failed and most of the other plotters had been arrested, including the Force Commander, John Bangura. He was still flippant. He thought they were going to form the next Government. From the expression on his face, you could tell that he was becoming more pompous.

The next few hours saw a big dramaunfold in Byrne Lane. "Dombolo"'s house and ours, were surrounded by about four military trucks full of soldiers who came to capture him. They were all carrying guns. We were afraid it would be a gun battle.

"Come out," the sergeant shouted. "No need trying to escape because you are surrounded."

"Dombolo" came out of his house with his hands up. Some soldiers jumped from the walls behind him, arrested him, and kicked his backside inside the truck. At that moment all I was thinking about was what he had done to my friend Alex Cotey, a few months before. Now it was his turn. Eventually, all the coup plotters were rounded up, including the Force Commander, John Bangura, the then Minister of Information, Ibrahim Taqi, Minister of Finance, Dr Forna. Army officers like Major Jawara, Abu Noah and Corporal Foday Sankoh were all charged with treason, and tried. Lieutenant Harold "Dombolo", Abu

Noah, and Foday Sankoh were sentenced to long term imprisonment, to be later pardoned by Siaka Stevens after serving a few years. Those considered being his closest rivals, and a political threat to his position: Dr Forna, Ibrahim Taqi, John Bangura, and Major Jawara were all executed. This was the beginning of political killings in Sierra Leone for the first time under the A.P.C rule of Siaka Stevens.

I will never forget that morning when it was announced that these men had been executed. It was a quiet and gloomy day; the atmosphere in Freetown was not good. Who would have known that Ibrahim Taqi and Dr, Forna, the very people who helped to build the A.P.C. party would have been killed by Siaka Stevens? Not only that, the very Force Commander, John Bangura, had caused his own death by installing Siaka Stevens as Prime Minister. He signed his own death warrant. This is when we say in Krio, "If ah bin know," meaning, "If I had known."

To secure his position after these executions, Siaka Stevens declared the country a Republic. Further fortifying his position, he created a militia he called I.S.U (Internal Security Unit). After this we began to see the spread of ammunition in the country. Political thugs were sent to places like Russia, Cuba, East Germany and other socialist countries. In fact that was the type of ideological government he wanted to bring in Sierra Leone which, I am quite sure, he himself didn't understand. Although his government was supposed to be a national unity government, he systematically got rid of the main S.L.P.P members of his government and installed his own stalwarts. Freedom of speech was not as tolerated as

Sir Albert had tolerated the Press, especially the official Press of S.L.P.P (Unity) edited by Sam Metzger, one of the finest Journalists in Sierra Leone at that time, in my opinion. People were frightened to talk politically to one another because you did not know who was an agent for "Pa Sheki" as the Prime Minister" was called. Political appointees, such as High Commissioners and Ambassadors were all party stalwarts. Generally speaking, people who are appointed to these posts should be people with distinguished careers in public life or business in the country, people like Dr Davidson-Nicol. But under Siaka Stevens and Dr General Saidu Momoh, we had somebody like a school-mate of mine who, when I was in the third form, was in the 5th form. He never had any distinguished career in public life or business. The only public life he had, as far as I know, was that of lead singer in a band called, "Eddie and the West Africans High life Band." He ended up as High Commissioner in a well known advanced country. There were many of his kind who benefited during the presidency of Siaka Stevens and Momoh. Some fell by the wayside, not lucky enough. Some of them would end up doing Environmental Engineering jobs, if you know what I mean, in England.

Under these two regimes our country was becoming violent with lots of political killings. We saw the execution of First Vice-President, Francis Minah, a brilliant Lawyer in Freetown when I was working in the Law Courts. His execution took place under Momoh's presidency. We also saw the brutal killing of Sam Bangura, the Governor of the Bank of Sierra Leone, under Siaka Stevens. A Trinidadian called Victor Bruce was appointed Governor of the Bank in succession to Sam Bangura. He also died mysteriously in Sierra Leone. Meanwhile our currency was deteriorating fast. For example in 1971, when I left Sierra Leone, the exchange rate was two Leones to one pound sterling. As the years went by, I was told that you had to take a suitcase to the bank to withdraw the equivalent of a few thousand British pounds. The country was deteriorating fast. In previous years, if you were not within the rank of a top judge or lawyer, you would not be appointed to the rank of Speaker of the House of Representatives. Hence we had people like Sir Salako Benka-Coker, Sir Henry Lightfoot-Boston, Sir Banja Tejan-Sie and other distinguished Sierra Leoneans serving in these senior capacities.

Chapter 12

Living in England

On 17th September, 1971, I left Freetown for London, stopping at Algiers in transit. I waited for three hours before boarding an Air France flight for London Heathrow. On arrival at Heathrow Airport, I went through all the immigration formalities without any problem, and went on to the baggage hall to collect my suitcase, which I treasured so much. In fact I only got rid of it in 2002. I had put an emotional attachment to it, as an item made in Sierra Leone.

I met my brother-in-law, Issa Bureh in the arrival area, a senior member of the Bureh Clan in Sierra Leone, brother of the late Kandeh Bureh snr, and a cabinet minister in both Sir Milton and Sir Albert Margai's government who also served a spell in Siaka Stevens's Government. Issa arrived in England in the early 50s as an ex-schoolmaster from Freetown. He is married to my sister Beatrice Koryeh, the pillar of strength in my family.

From London Heathrow he took me to Euston Station to board a train to Manchester. The escalators were much bigger than the one in Kingsway Stores so stepping on one of them frightened me a bit, especially the one in Euston. Issa treated me to a first class ticket for my first rail journey that lasted about three hours. On arrival in Manchester Picadilly, we took a taxi to West Didsbury where I was warmly greeted by my sister Koryeh whom I had not seen for about ten years, apart from photographs. With them were my nephew, Billy Lahai, and niece ,Maria, and Issa's cousin, Barbara Lewis, our "Auntie Babs". We quickly settled down to the usual welcome meal.

I was already a week late for college, so my friend, Sam Coker, who played a significant role in getting me a place in college, had to come and collect me on Sunday to take me to Bolton to start college the next day. Koryeh gave me £20 which, in 1971, was worth a lot. Sam Coker had already arranged a rented room with his landlords, an Indian couple called Mr. and Mrs. Shah, who also welcomed me. My address was 48 Bromwich Street, a popular location with foreign students, especially those from Africa. Most Sierra Leoneans who were at Bolton have lived on that street. The main colleges in Bolton included the Bolton Technical College main building at Manchester Road, and Annex in Folds Road; the college of Higher Education and the Bolton College of Arts at Bromwich Street, and the Bolton Institute of Technology, a College for Higher Education in the Town Centre on Dean Road.

Soon after I arrived in Bolton, I found out that Bolton Wanderers, a football club I liked so much since I was in Freetown trained on practice grounds near my house. When I heard Nat Lofthouse's name I thought this was an opportunity to see him, not knowing that he had already retired. Instead, I was able to see the stars of the day, the Great Jimmy Amfield, the manager at that time, and players like Peter Reid, John Byron, Sam Allardyce, and Paul Jones. I watched them in training, and also occasionally when playing at Burden Park, the Wanderers Football Grounds at Manchester Road.

I soon started college and I can vividly remember my first day, I felt so cold, with tears running down my eyes.

I said to myself: Lord, what have I let myself in for? Then braced myself thinking:you have fallen into the sea, now you have to swim, except that I can't. Sam Coker kindly accompanied me, and introduced me to the Principal before taking me to my class to start work in earnest. I worked especially hard to make up for the lost week, and luckily every assigned subject was familiar, with the exception of statistics.

I was working towards the Ordinary National Diploma in Business Studies and Administration. The subjects I took included accounting, commerce, economics, geography, law, structure and organisation of business, and office administration. Thanks to my earlier schooling in Sierra Leone, I could cope quite well with all of these subjects, excelling in economics and geography. For this I will say a special thank you to Mrs. Caroline Roy-Macaulay, a former teacher at Collegiate School. I also did well in law because of my practical experience gained whilst working in the Masters Office at the Law Courts in Freetown. I was able to understand and relate to the different legal terminology in criminal, tort, contract and property law. Soon I started to make friends. At first there were only two other black students in the class, one from Cameroon and the other from Uganda. They had lived in England for many years and were behaving and speaking like white men, too artificial for my comfort as a newly arrived African. Luckily I was joined by a great guy, Sylvester Tram, from Nigeria. He was always proud that he came from the Mid-West. He had wanted to go back to Nigeria when the winter cold got into him for the first few days, but, like me, he decided to stick it out. Straight away we became good buddies because we had so much in common. He had received some commercial education in Nigeria and could type very well. We learnt a great deal together. He lived just a few hundred yards from me. On my way to college, I would call for him and we would go together. We studied together, went out together when the occasion arose. Like me, he could cook quite well especially Egusi Soup which we would eat with ground rice.

One day in college my friend, Olu Coker, came to look for me carrying his usual smile.

"Humble," he shouted, "I've found a part-time job for you at Barlow and Jones, Falcon Mill where I'm working." They were located at Halliwell Road, going towards the northern area of Bolton. At first I said to him,

"Olu this will be difficult, I have to study, and have too many projects to do."

He said to me "You backside, you want to just depend on your sister, Koryeh, to be giving you £20 every week? Is that how you want to survive in this England?"

"No" I replied. "What are the hours of work?"

"4.30 p.m.-9.30 p.m. You finish college at 4 p.m. and in twenty minutes you will be at work,". he replied. Olu was a lovely man and very helpful. By that time, he was well established around town. I therefore, trusted him and said "Alright."

He introduced me to the manager, Alan Aspin, and the supervisor, Jack Hargreaves. They agreed I should start work the next day. Bolton, like Lancashire, was at the centre of a thriving textile industry with thousands of factory workers spinning, weaving and dyeing cotton; I could not help but think about my visit to Makeni. This particular firm specialised in spinning. I cleaned the machines on Saturday mornings and in the evenings after college I got bobbins and fixed spinning wheels for the women. I enjoyed every bit of it, and looked forward to my first pay packet. When I received and opened it, I counted £40. I jumped for joy, and when I told Olu about my first wage packet after work, he said to me, "I told you so; now you can relieve your sister from her £20 weekly allowance to you."

I rang Koryeh, and told her about my new job, and that I wouldn't be coming that weekend as I had to do some flat-hunting. I wanted to live independently. This was no problem for Olu, as he took me to a Russian landlord who had two houses in Bromwich Street, and two in Bradford Road nearby. I became his new tenant in flat number 66 upstairs with a big and comfortable room for which I only paid £5 weekly, and we shared the kitchen and bathroom for the two of us on that floor; a Jamaican man called Rupert lived in the other, and I recall Sunday mornings when we usually enjoyed the mouth-watering smell of chicken and rice wafting from the kitchen as he showed off his culinary expertise. By midday after taking one or two tots of Jamaican white rum, he would sit down, and tell me about the good old days in Jamaica, and England. I found it useful to listen to people like him who helped broaden my worldly experience. Another friend, Dotun, studied law and English "A" levels at the main college at Manchester Road, and although we sometimes worked together, I made it plain to him that I could only help him with the law essays as I was doing law myself.

One day, Dotun came home late at around 11 p.m., knocked on my door; luckily I was not asleep.

"Tucker," he shouted. I opened my door. "Thanks for that law essay last week, look at it, I had a "B", man, you understand this law."

"I like law, it's my favourite subject," I replied, "no problem." Considering my past experience in the courts at home, I often regret not pursuing that noble profession in the end.

The following week, he came early, knocked on my door, asked me to come and chat having just finished smoking "weed". I could smell it although he tried to spray the room with air freshener to disguise the distinctive odour. Anyway, I didn't say a word, pretending that I couldn't smell anything. Next thing he said to me, "I came home early today and cooked some good Egusi soup - will you try some"? I consented as saliva filled my mouth in anticipation. When we finished eating, I complemented him on his cooking. After a short while he brought the law books out and showed me another piece of work they gave him and, as usual, we did it together. He was a nice fellow and I found it difficult to refuse him anything. After that he disappeared from the house for a few weeks, which worried me as he hadn't hinted he would be away for so long. I later discovered that his rent arrears for two months had forced him to dodge the landlord, Ivan. I came to know about this when Ivan complained to me. Ivan was a big tall man. I used to call him "Ivan De Terrible" because of his height, and size resembling one of these wartime veteran soldiers. Whenever he came for the rent, he would sit down to chat for a few minutes. During one such chat, one day, Dotun appeared unexpectedly. The landlord demanded his rent for two months, and soon it turned into a big argument, which ended in a fight between a huge and tall Ivan, and a smaller Dotun. I quickly separated them, and got an agreement from Dotun to pay up on a certain date. It felt like my good turn for the day as two friends should not have been fighting like that.

I soon became a supporter of Manchester United FC and often went to Old Trafford, to watch Bobby Charlton, and Georgie Best. On one memorable Saturday I witnessed a great game they played against Sheffield United using other great players in the team, such as Brian Kidd, Willie Morgan, and Alex Stepney, under their manager Frank O'Farrell. But I could not help but admire Tony Currie and Trevor Hockney of Sheffield United too. Later on when I moved to Manchester and lived in Didsbury, and Fallowfield, I regularly watched Manchester City at Main Road, fielding great players like Francis Lee, Colin Bell, Mike Summerbee, and Joe Corrigan. I really enjoyed those early years in England, watching English football. Sadly, the trend in the game these days is money, money, money, spent on players, some of whom are injury-prone, and do not even live up to the high expectations.

Chapter 13

Family life

I was surprised at the speed at which I adjusted to my new host country, and did not spend time pining for my earlier activities at home. Time seemed to pass so quickly that I had to run to stay still.

From Bolton I moved permanently to Manchester, and stayed with my sister Beatrice, and husband Issa temporarily until I got my own flat at Old Landsdowne Road in West Didsbury. I continued to attend the Stockport College of Technology in Greater Manchester where I spent two years doing a Higher National Diploma in Personnel Management. In order to be able to finance my college fees and maintain myself domestically, I managed to get an evening job in Picadilly Manchester at a massive hotel called Grande Hotel at Aytown Street, owned by Sir Charles Forte, one of the hotel magnates at that time. Amongst my new friends when I first arrived in Manchester were two sisters Rosamond and Rosalinda Thomas, and not forgetting Margaret George whom I knew previously at Murray Town. I thus survived until the end of the two years of full time studies.

Naturally, I then felt that the world was my oyster. Feeling relaxed one day I set off from Stockport to do some window shopping. On arriving in Manchester Picadilly I headed straight for Debenhams. As usual, I went to the records department to buy one or two long playing records (LPs), which I knew I could afford at £3 - £4 each. As I stood there looking for bargains, I spotted a tall beautiful lady looking at records herself. I immediately thought: what a beauty! and felt a strong urge to "go and talk to her" - to chat her up. With perfect timing, and synchronisation she selected some LPs as I did also. As she approached the cashier I stayed behind her as the inner voice kept on coming to me ,"Go on, talk to her." As we left the cashier, I plucked up enough courage to approach her. "Hello!!" I said. She replied "hello" ever so politely, the dimples on her cheeks sent tingles down my spine. Feeling inspired, and besotted I made bold to introduce myself. She responded favourably in like manner telling me her name, Joan Celestine. Still in a trance I asked, "Where are you going to now?" There was clearly some chemistry between us; my effrontery worked, and she volunteered her plan.

"I'm going to Boots the chemists at Corporation Street."

I did not need an invitation. "Shall I accompany you?" I asked. Without any hesitation she replied, "I don't mind." I most certainly did not either, so off we went together; I did not even feel a bit nervous though excited. After buying what she wanted, and before parting company, we exchanged addresses and our telephone numbers.

I believe that meeting Joan was sheer destiny because she came at the right time when I had no special friendship with any woman, and a serious relationship seemed timely after my studies. She lived in the nurses hostel at the Royal Eye Hospital in Manchester, within easy reach of Didsbury. We started to telephone each other, and exchange visits, and I soon discovered she came from the island of Grenada in the West Indies.

We had a pay telephone in the hall way of my flat for residents' use, but I was out when she rang soon after. The lady who answered the call unfortunately had a crush although I had not encouraged her when we spoke once in a while. Totally, and without any justification she said to Joan, "Why are you ringing him? Didn't he tell you that I'm his girlfriend?" She never told me about Joan's phone call and what she said to her until Joan told me herself. I quickly put her right about the real position, and told Joan not to let that worry her. To prevent a repeat of this mischievous trick, I changed my strategy, and decided to arrange with my former landlord in Bromwich Street, Bolton, for a flat. He agreed I could take the top flat in his house. It's very rare for a foreigner to live with an English family as their tenant, but because I once lived with them, and we enjoyed a good relationship, I was privileged to be welcomed back. My friend, Pat, liked Joan and when I told her about the telephone incident she said to me, "Try not to give this lady a miss, she suits you." She even asked her boyfriend, Ayo, who came from London every weekend to see her, to take me to Bolton the following weekend.

Friday night I got my things ready, went over to my landlady in Clyde Road to pay my rent up to date and told her that I got a job in Bolton. Coincidentally, and out of the blue, Allan Aspin, my former manager in Bolton, rang and asked me if I wanted a summer job, which was a Godsend. Saturday came and Ayo was there to whisk me off to Bolton.

I spent the whole of Summer 1975 in Bolton. Joan came to visit me regularly until I eventually moved back to Manchester to live in Chorlton-Cum-Hardy with a Ghanaian friend, Samuel Donkoh, who had a spare room in his Council House. Joan found this much more convenient as it was just about 15-20 minutes walk from her hospital in Manchester. By now, I knew she was definitely for me, and thought myself lucky.

My good fortune continued, and I landed a job as a clerical officer in the Civil Service Department of Employment, working in the Benefits Agency. We moved to Ladybarn in Fallowfield Manchester, and lived together with an Englishman, Dave Kemp, and his wife Anne. We occupied the second floor of the house. Whilst there we got married in 1976 and in July 1977 we had our first child, Joe, named after my putative father Joseph. A few months after the birth of Joe, we decided to buy our own house. In fact it was just a few hundred yards away from where we lived, which was good because we liked the environment, and were not far from both of our jobs, or Manchester Picadilly. I worked for the Department of Employment for seven years before deciding to go to University to Study for a Political Science degree. I was given study leave without pay; obviously I knew I was not coming back. I started the course after we had our first daughter Jasmine, who was only one year old. This was the beginning of a struggle for me because Manchester City Council Education Department refused me a grant for the first year explaining that I had completed both the Higher Education and the Higher National Diploma courses, so did not qualify.

I was determined to even fight the then Head of Department, and many of the lecturers pleaded on my behalf. I wrote to many charitable organizations to help me for the first year. It was a waste of time. I decided to take my case to the Black Political Radicals starting with Professor Gus John, now lecturer at a Scottish University, who happened to be my wife's countryman from Grenada. Being an active campaigner for race equality in Manchester, he embraced my case with some determination, contacting his friend in London, a well known journalist and broadcaster, Darcus, and Editor of a magazine, 'Race Today'. He published details of my case in one edition with the aim of giving this injustice as much publicity as possible. In the end, Manchester City wrote to me, stating that they were looking into my case again. Imagine my determination and all the stress that followed. Despite that I progressed to the second year of the course, much to my relief, whilst most of my friends did not make it.

Six months into my second year, our second daughter Jean-Marie Aminata was born. Now the real struggle began, with three kids. Money was tight. Joan was now the only bread winner in the family. I paid for that course for the first and second years before seeking alternative outside help. I went to my bank and negotiated a loan. Luckily the assistant bank manager, a Sierra Leonean, Abu Turay, a family friend who knew about my situation and determination, used his influence to get the loan. I was able to pay the fees, and enrol, and did not agonize as to whether it was nepotism or a bad thing to 'get a leg up.'

Luckily, the Council made their decision in my favour, and sent me money. I was entitled to over £3000. The first thing I did was to pay back the bank loan and buy some political theory books which I wanted to keep. At last some joy came to the family after paying some outstanding bills. My kids were too young to understand all that was going on. At this point I must mention my good friend, Peter Ekoku, a Nigerian law student He came to my rescue so many times, even when he had problems of his own. It seemed obvious and appropriate that we should invite him to act as Jean-Marie's Godfather at her christening.

I sailed through to the final year, and got my degree. The Graduation Ceremony held at the Free Trade Hall, Manchester with much pomp and pageantry involved the Academics in their ceremonial robes. One by one graduands were awarded their degrees according to their faculties. Finally, the Social Science faculty took the stage, and as I got up from my seat, I could see tears running from Joan's eyes as she remembered all the struggle and hard work I had endured in order to reach this stage. As I stepped up to receive my award, I noticed, in particular, the loud applause coming from Dr. Roberts, the Head of Faculty, Dr. Jules Townsend, and Dr. Paul Kennedy, specialist in Third World politics. These were lecturers who knew the difficulties I had to overcome before graduation.

I continued with my studies, completing a post-graduate course to specialize in Careers Guidance Education and Training thereby responding to a demand for more black people at the time. This was a nine-month course, and as soon as I completed it, I got a temporary job with the Education Department Crown Square, working for the Careers Service. Ironically this was the very Education Department that had messed my life up in the beginning. I could not believe I ended up working for them.

I failed to secure a permanent job in Manchester, so I decided to move up to London in January 1988 to a more permanent job, working for Brent Education Careers Service. After privatization in 1996, it is now run by a private Education Company called Nord Anglia. Currently as the Lifetime Careers Limited Brent and Harrow, an amalgamation of two Boroughs, Brent and Harrow.

Joan and me!

Chapter 14

Tracing my Congolese roots

I had always had a deep desire to discover my roots in the Congo. For years, whilst growing up in Sierra Leone, I wrote articles for publicity in newspapers, and the Ministry of Information, sent requests through Radio Brazzaville, a very popular station in Sierra Leone. Nearly every young teenager listened to sounds from Brazzaville at 5:45 p.m. each day, including my two friends: Osho and Balogun Coker, and sometimes my good friend, Prince Shyllon, but none was as fanatical about Congolese music as I. In those days, you had bands in Congo Kinshasa, like Franco and the O.K. Jazz, Negro Success with Bavon-Marie Marie and Bohlem. In Brazzaville you had bands like Bantu De La Capital, and Pa Pa Noel, and Bantu Jazz, not forgetting Papa Wemba, of course. Anyway, the communication barrier proved the greatest problem in tracing my roots.

I got quite close to succeeding around 1965-66 when the football champions of Brazzaville went to Sierra Leone to play mighty Blackpool. I strongly believed that by mingling with the visitors I would get some answers. They played to a packed National Stadium, and the game ended in a draw. I attempted to contact the Brazzaville team at the Brookfields Hotel where the host team held a reception for them, but could not communicate with most of them as they only spoke French. But I managed to talk to their left-winger, Desire Ngu in English. I visited him twice in the hotel before they departed, and told him about my mother Sissy, and other family members in the Congo, but his promise to help proved futile. I met him again in Brazzaville, years later.

The final breakthrough came in May 1988, just after I had moved to London, leaving my family in Manchester. I lived with a Sierra Leonean, Mr. Sema Phillip Bangura and his wife, Aminata, in Mayfield Road, Hornsey, North London in the Borough of Haringey. I had received a letter from my mother, Sissy, earlier containing two complimentary cards, one of which carried the name of Madame Veronique. Sissy explained in her letter how her next door neighbour, an Ivory Coast Diplomat named Mr. Motcho, became very interested after listening to her life history, and had promised to help her trace her roots. Fortuitously for us, Motcho regularly attended conferences together with delegates from most of the French-speaking countries in Africa. He undertook to talk to any delegate from the Congo during his next conference.

It was as if God was working in mysterious ways because not too long after that Mr. Motcho attended a conference, and took the opportunity to relate Sissy's story to two female delegates from the Congo. They too found it fascinating, and were smart enough to give him their complimentary cards to bring back to Sissy in Freetown so that she could keep in touch with them in the Congo. Sissy did one better, and sent the cards to me, so I decided it would be sensible to write to Madame Veronique laying emphasis on the name Christopher Williams, and Fatouma, my grandparents, drawing attention to the town of Quesso. Struck by the timescale of the 1920s, Madame Veronique found my letter very interesting, and decided to do something for this family, starting that very day.

Amazingly, her house stood but a few yards from Sissy's sister Beatrice Tamod's in Quenza, Brazzaville whom she interviewed initially as she stepped out.

Mr Tamod was a surgeon in the military in Congo, and at that time Grandma Fatouma lived in Quenza with daughter, Beatrice. One of my cousins, Christopher Williams Tamod, a young lieutenant in the Congolese Army, was named after Granddad. News of the ancestoral search caused both thrill and excitement within the family in Quenza. To add to this, my first cousin Rosaline Tamod Monthault, then the welfare and social attaché at the Democratic Republic of the Congo Embassy in Paris, visiting on holidays, also became involved. She wrote me a letter from Brazzaville introducing herself and the rest of the family in Congo, and promised to contact me as soon as she returned to Paris.

True to her word, I got a phone call from Paris a week later: "It's me Rosalie," she said, "I'm back in Paris. I will be in London on Saturday, arriving at Gatwick Airport at 11 a.m". This came as a most pleasing surprise to me because everything had happened so quickly, and moreover the rest of my family had just moved from Manchester to join me in London. When I told my wife about the phone call, and that we were having a visitor the following Saturday, she understandably worried more because the house was not properly furnished, and felt we would be humiliated if a lady of that status saw our living conditions. I reassured her about the real importance of a family visit by a long lost relative arising from the rapid events of the past few weeks thus replacing her worry with justifiable excitement.

On Saturday I went to Gatwick, and met Rosalie, and daughter Marthylda. We had no difficulty recognising each other because we'd previously exchanged photographs. As soon as she saw me she pointed to me, and I did the same. We embraced each other; she greeted me in French, and I returned the welcome in English. She spoke little English. Luckily the daughter spoke English, and acted as interpreter. At times like this I often wondered if it would have been much more useful to have spent the five years I did at school studying Latin, learning French instead. Latin to me seemed a waste of time, and we would have been far better off with practical Languages, such as French, Spanish, German, Italian and Portuguese. Anyway, we came home, and were welcomed by my family, and we had lunch together. After lunch we sat in the living room, and I showed her a picture of Sissy. She burst into tears because of the resemblance between Sissy, and her Grandma Fatoumata. She rang her mum Beatrice in the Congo to tell her about her fantastic family reunion in London speaking Lingala which is the lingua franca of the Congolese; French is the official language.

For me, Lingala is the most beautiful and romantic language in the world. That's why I am so obsessed with Congolese music. As I was listening to Rosalie talking to her mum on the phone I could tell from her expression that she was trying to describe how Sissy was just the spitting image of Grandma Fatoumata. Saturday was our usual shopping day. Living in Brockley, we would usually go to Peckham, which was just ten minutes drive from our place. Peckham is predominately multi-cultural; therefore all kinds of foodstuffs were catered for – African, Caribbean, and Asian. Rosalie insisted she wanted to accompany us to the market in Peckham. She liked it. She bought a bunch of flowers for Joan. On Sunday we went on the usual sightseeing around London – Trafalgar Square, Buckingham Palace, Downing Street, Parliament, Regents Park, and so on. We had a good day out, came home, and I prepared the dinner. After dinner we sat down to listen to some Congolese music. She was amazed at the large collection of records I had accumulated over the years. Her favourite singer was Koffie Olomide, one of the leading Congolese singers. Apparently Koffie's mother originally came from Sierra Leone, and settled in Kinshasa. On the contrary, my mother came from Brazzaville, and settled in Sierra Leone.

Rosalie told us about her family in Brazzaville. Of Beatrice's children, she is the eldest, followed by Henriette, who is married to Mr Gabrielle Nzambila, Mary Noelle-Flfi, Valerie Jose, Christopher Williams Tamod, Dodo, Edmonde, and Marius - six females and two males.

In turn, I told her about our own family of three males and three females; Beatrice Koryeh the eldest, who lives in Manchester, myself, Edward Tunde Woode, who lives in the U.S, Emelia Sarah, Emmanuel Lati, and Druscilla Oloh. Emmanuel lives in the US whilst Emelia and Druscilla live in Freetown.

Rosalie loved Peckham so much that she asked Joan to accompany her back there the following Tuesday. She wanted to shop so that she could come and prepare a Congolese meal for us. I said, "What dish are you going to prepare?" She replied, "Dongor Dongor." Later I found out it was okra soup which is also a favourite dish in Sierra

Leone. As I found out later when I went to Brazzaville in December 1989, Sierra Leone and Congo do have similar dishes. For example in Sierra Leone one of our main dishes is cassava leaves, a vegetable sauce. In Congo it is also their main dish, and they call it 'saca-saca'. They prepare theirs differently from the way we do in Sierra Leone. Rosalie and my wife went to Peckham, and did the shopping, and Joan could not help but notice that Rosalie's elegant beauty did not go unadmired by other shoppers. I noticed the same thing when I later visited her in Paris where she is a very respectable lady locally.

I virtually rushed back from work the next day to enjoy Rosalie's cuisine. Unexpectedly, during the meal she suggested that my mum should travel to the Congo so she could meet the rest of the family she had not seen for over fifty-five years; she would travel via Paris so that Rosalie would have the chance to meet her for the first time. I could barely wait until after the meal to call Sissy to tell her the good news. I instructed her to go to the British High Commission in Freetown to start applying for her visas.

To digress a little, Sissy got a one-year visa to London quite easily as she had been to England before when stayed with us in Manchester for over a year. However, the French Embassy refused to issue a transit visa for a week via Paris to Brazzaville. I could not contain my fury as I wrote to the visa office at the French Embassy in Freetown seeking a reason for refusing a transit visa to a sixty-five year old lady who merely wanted to visit her Diplomat niece in Paris for a few days before proceeding to the Congo. Venting my anger, and in an attempt to embarrass the official further I said, "You white people like to go to the Caribbean, Africa and sun tan yourselves; but when it comes to black people wanting to come to your part of the world, even on a visit, or in Sissy's case just in transit, you make all kinds of fuss." Anyway, they didn't have the courtesy to reply.

At the end of a very enjoyable week I waved Rosalie and Marthylda goodbye at Gatewick Airport as they left for Paris. Sissy arrived safely at London Heathrow Airport by British Caledonian Airways a week later, and my colleague at work called Cleveland Bartram volunteered to collect her in his car with me. We came home where she was happy to see us once more. I did not have time to apply for a transit visa at the French Embassy in London so we had to take a gamble, and let her go to Charles de Gaulle Airport, and then apply for a transit visa. Rosalie met Sissy at the Airport, and helped to settle a little dispute at immigration after which they granted a transit visa for two weeks en route to Brazzaville. Sissy stayed with Rosalie, and Marthylda for a week and the following week she travelled to the Congo by Air France. The whole family had travelled the short distance from the family home in Quenza to greet her on arrival at Maya-Maya airport in Brazzaville. The atmosphere in the family house resembled the return of the "prodigal son," a big feast had been prepared, with neighbours, relatives and friends celebrating, especially Fatoumata, my grandmother, who was overwhelmed with emotion to see her long-lost daughter after over fifty years. Sissy was also full of joy to be reunited with her sister, Beatrice, and a half-sister called Neneh, born long after Sissy left for Sierra Leone, from a different father.

Sadly before her return many months later, tragedy was to strike in the family. Our cousin, Mayoma, who was a prominent citizen in Quenza was involved in a plane crash around Sepetember/October 1989. She and her husband were taking their daughter for schooling in Paris. The Air France flight they were travelling in took off from Maya-Maya airport, was apparently hijacked by terrorists, and crashed somewhere in the Sahara Desert. The crash site was only discovered months later. I felt particularly sad because a few weeks before this tragic accident I got a letter from Sissy in Brazzaville telling me about my wonderful cousin, Mayoma, who couldn't wait to see me, and had been asking her to try and persuade me to come to Brazzaville as soon as possible. Mayoma was a very wealthy lady, as well as being very influential in Brazzaville. The family went into full mourning after this tragedy; the whole family and close friends had to wear the same clothes – cotton material of dark shade. Normally, some wear it for six months and some for a year, depending on how close you are to the deceased person. This same tradition is also practised in Sierra Leone to mark the period of mourning. So many members of the Congolese family wanted Sissy to go and spend time with them. Amongst the first she spent time with was the Nzambila family in Point Noire, the other main city in the Congo. Mr Nzambila is the husband of Henriette, niece of Sissy. She stayed with them for a few months. Henriette and Sissy looked so much alike they were like identical twins. Everywhere they went in Point Noire or in Brazzaville, people would ask Henriette whether that was her mother. Eventually she became so fed up about this, and most times she would simply answer "yes". In fact I had a taste of this as well in London years later in the Year 2000 when Henriette visited us. My wife, and I took her to Peckham, and met a family friend from Sierra Leone who grew up with Sissy in Hastings. Before I could open my mouth to introduce Henriette, this friend, Mr Alahkor, said "This woman looks so much like Sissy when she was younger". I then said to my wife Joan, "You hear what he said? She looks like Sissy." And I also turned to Henriette and said, "Do you hear what he said to me? He said you look like Mama Lillian." She just smiled. She'd heard that before many times. Sissy stayed in Brazzaville for almost two years, and could understand, and speak Lingala a little. The family, initiated plans for her to remain in Brazzaville, and even went to the extent of offering her a small house, an offer which she refused after careful consideration. She felt part of Sierra Leone where she had lived for so long; besides, she did not want to abandon her children, and grandchildren to go and settle in the Congo. She therefore, promised them that if all went well she would be paying them regular visits. However, she has not been back since, and it is most unlikely that she will go again, considering her age.

Les Diables Noires, Champions of Congo-Brazzaville

L to R, Madam Veronique, next to my Mum's sisters, Madam Beatric Tamod and Neneh)

Second from left my Aunt. Beatrice and in red dress my mother Janet

My mum (in red) on arrival at Quenza, being welcomed by the family

Third from the left, my late cousin and far right Aunty Neneh

Chapter 15

Visit to Brazzaville

For many years I dreamt that I would one day visit Congo-Brazzaville, partly to trace my origins, and any relatives who were still alive, and partly because of my enormous appetite for Congolese music. After Sissy's visit to Brazzaville in 1988, I came under lots of pressure to do likewise. At last, in November1989, I made the decision to go on holidays to the Congo. The next thing was to search for suitable flights, and I soon found out that Air France and Air Afrique were very expensive. Thanks to some friendly advice I settled for travelling on the Russian Airlines Aeroflot for £454. The only problem was that I would have to travel to Malta via Moscow, and via Doula in Cameroon. However, my passport was still in Freetown awaiting renewal, but luckily a school mate of mine, Ade Jones was the Welfare, and Passport officer at the Sierra Leone Embassy in London, and for a small fee of £5 or so and with a passport photograph issued me with a travelling certificate. Similarly, I faxed all details to my cousin's husband, Mr Gabriel Nzambila, and in a matter of days, I got a certificate of entry to the Congo from their immigration department, delivered by DHL Parcel delivery.

I then visited the World Sports Supporters Club near Oxford Street, and paid my friend, Isatu, (she is everybody's friend!!) an officer working for this agency who told me to collect the ticket in a few days. So everything was arranged, and settled.

On a Tuesday around 10 a.m. I boarded the massive Aeroflot airtcraft at London Heathrow. The flight took between three to four hours to arrive in Moscow, enough time to make friends with a Cameroonian called Simon, sitting next to me, a civil engineer. Moscow airport had four inches of snow, and felt extremely cold. We went to the main airport terminal to clear immigration under tight Security, and were to stay in Moscow overnight to travel to Brazzaville the next morning. The airline had arranged a tour of Moscow for that night, for which we had to pay £20, so we had the opportunity to see all the important places in the city. Halfway along the route. the bus broke down. The tour guide, who spoke fluent English, apologised for this and explained to us that all bus drivers were trained mechanics, and in no time the bus was on the move again. At the end of a very enjoyable, and educational trip, we went back to the transit area of the airport for a meal, followed by television. Some passengers slept on settees.

We departed Moscow in the morning in a plane packed full with Congolese and Cameroonians bound for Malta. We arrived safely in Malta for a three- hour refuelling stop spent in transit within the airport, and about six hours later we arrived in Doula where I parted company with Simon. I felt very happy to be once again on African soil, and spent my three hours in transit thinking about Roger Miller and the Cameroon Football team, and famous musicians Moni Bale and Ebua Lotin before we took off for the last leg of 30-35 minutes to Brazzaville.

I was wearing a black striped suit, feeling tall and elegant. When the plane landed at Maya-Maya airport, Mr Nzambila walked out to greet me on the tarmac, and accompanied me to the VIP lounge where most of my relatives were waiting to greet me, including Sissy, my mother. The lounge was packed full; both my aunties, Beatrice and Neneh ,were there, my cousins Marie Noell-Fifi, Valerie Jose, Edmonde, Marius, young lieutenant Christopher Williams Tamod, and Dodo were all there. I spotted my mother standing with my other cousin, Colonel Youla Diendonne, but not in uniform. Nevertheless, many soldiers and police saluted him leaving me in no doubt of his senior rank. Now, everybody wanted to speak to me in English, though I must confess I could not understand what some of them were trying to say. Congo is a Francophone country whereas Sierra Leone is Anglophone. Of the lot, only Mr Nzambila, and my cousin Marius spoke proper English. Nevertheless, I did manage to somehow communicate with all of them, even if it meant using some form of sign language. Anyway, Mr Nzambila and Colonel Youla took Sissy and me in their car, a Mercedes Benz. The house in Quenza was only about 15-20 minutes drive from Maya-Maya. When we arrived, the house was packed with visitors, and other relatives who were not able to come to the airport to meet me. These included the great old lady herself, my grandmother, Fatoumata. Even though I figured her age to be between eighty-six and ninety years, she looked so good - strong and healthy. She hugged and kissed me four times on both sides of the cheek, and kept looking at me and crying all the time. I kept on looking from her to Sissy; they looked so much alike,

By this time food was already prepared. My mouth watered as I realised they had prepared my favourite home sauce, "cassava leaves" or "jakitomboi" known in the Congo as "saca-saca". Whilst they were arranging the seating order, my favourite band, OK Jazz, played a familiar song on the air, which I sang word for word even though I could not understand the language. They were amazed to see me dance, and sing, and my mother told them that, more than any of her other children, I was the one that had the pure Congolese blood in me. I felt proud. After a short prayer by Auntie Beatrice we sat down to eat with a resounding "bon appetit." I noticed that the side dish contained pineapple or "ananas" in French, and these were so big! I never saw such big pineapples in all my life.

I quickly learned that apart from the Agro-industry, Congo-Brazzaville ran a very impressive timber industry. Situated in the Equatorial Forest Region, the country produced very good mahogany timber for use by their master craftsmen, carpenters and joiners who produced first class wall cabinets, chairs, settees, and tables. I was told that American tourists sometimes bought furniture in Congo-Brazzaville and shipped them to America, and could not understand our inability to derive similar benefit from our Forest Industry in Sierra Leone. The Congolese are a hardworking people, and everyone engaged in meaningful business activities during the day as market traders, small businessmen, or builders. At night they turned to all sorts of entertainment, including nightclubs, with local bands playing. Everywhere one could hear nothing but authentic Congolese music played in a masterful and professional manner.

I decided to start my second day in Brazzaville with a visit to Madam Veronique, as a thank you gesture for helping me to find my relatives. She had arranged for Mr. Emile Mouloudou, who had translated my letter from English to French when I first wrote to her, to meet with me. Later in the afternoon, Mr Nzambila collected me for a visit to his friend, the Mayor of Brazzaville who lived in a beautiful, and well kept house a few hundred yards from my family house in Quenza. The Mayor spoke English and we were able to converse easily whilst he entertained us to a lovely meal with his family. I found myself eating delicious cassava leaves again, and straight away started to feel more at home because Sierra Leone had much in common with Brazzaville. Given the choice to twin Freetown with any other city in Africa, it would be Brazzaville, I mused in between mouthfuls.

Soon I started making friends; Edmond Eyeletielet and Max Gangala both teenage schoolboys, became two faithful friends who were always with me until I left Brazzaville. I also met Doctor Termain Mouala, a Doctor of Economics and an immigrant from Sierra Leone. I was lucky that my family had kept the Sierra Leone name 'Williams', which was why it had been easy to trace them. For people like Doctor Mouala, his family did not keep the Sierra Leone name. I was told that he was the son, or grandson of Mr Thompson, my grandfather Christopher Williams's friend, with whom he travelled to Congo in the 1920s.

On my third day, my cousin, Marius, and his friend, Max Gangala, took me to a big open market called Makele Kele, where traders sold all sorts of goods especially arts and crafts carvings. One particular stall with some beautiful carvings caught my attention, and as we approached the young man in charge I said to Max, and Marius, "Don't let him know I'm from London otherwise he will charge us more, because these people always think customers from London, or America have lots of money." The young man heard us speaking English, and joined in the conversation shocking me with his fluency. It was a good thing he had not heard my earlier comment, or I would have felt so embarrassed. But my greatest surprise was yet to come when he revealed to me that he came from Sierra Leone and was called Alimamy. I could not believe such a coincidence, and tested him with a few choice phrases in Krio, which he passed with flying colours. My cousin and friend, Max, enjoyed listening to us talking something different from Lingala and English. Alimamy refused payment for the items I had selected costing about £100 saying, "T,ake them, they are presents from me," in exchange for the excitement of seeing his countryman who had brought lots of memories that afternoon. He took my address, and two days later came to the house in Quenza to meet my mother Sissy, and in fact brought more carvings for me. I felt even more embarrassed for having assumed he would overcharge me as a visitor from London.

Marius, and Max stayed with me the following day starting at the local market in Quenza. On the way, I spotted a very little man who did not look like any midget I had seen before, either in London or elsewhere, with short arms and legs, and usually a big head; with this man, everything was normal except that he was small. Marius explained that I had discovered a pigmy, taking me back to my school days at Collegiate School when my teacher, Mrs Caroline Roy-Macaulay, had taught us about pigmies of the Equatorial Forest in the Congo. Here was I meeting a pigmy for the first time instead of watching him on television in London on a special Horizon programme, learning how they live in the forest. Marius explained that the Government had a programme to encourage pigmies to integrate, and live normal lives with the rest of the country.

Continuing our stroll, Marius took me to see Pamelo Mounkaa's house not far from us. I knew him as the lead singer for a famous Brazzaville band called "Bantu De la Capital" and another band called "Bantu Jazz". Sadly, Pamelo was away in Paris, but Marious made up to me with a surprise invitation to a concert at the park that evening. We rushed home to a meal of 'bitter leaves and bologi and egusi soup,' that Sissy had already cooked as a treat for our hosts. 'Bitter leaf, bologi and egusi soup' is a favourite dish among the Krios in Sierra Leone. Bitter leaf grows all over the place in Congo, but they previously just used it for medicine. When Sissy cooked it, and they ate it, our relatives went crazy for the stuff.

I invited Sissy to join us for the evening concert which was preceded by some traditional masquerade dancing at the street corners resembling our 'ojeh', otherwise known as 'ogugu' in Sierra Leone. On arrival, the crowd was over 2000, and the stage was already set, with musicians fixing, and testing their instruments.

Soon Raphar, supported by his musicians, was on stage, and the great man, with his distinctive voice, played some fantastic music for over an hour. His deep patriotism could not be missed as he mentioned "Brazzaville" all the time. I recognised the next singer, and his music as Emeneya Kester who specialises in afro-rock with his band called, 'Victoria Eleison'. Being a very good dancer, the crowd went wild when he started playing, and dancing on stage. I could not control my legs and body either; people around me couldn't believe that a man from London could move to Congolese music like that. I couldn't resist dancing to a particular music as over 200 teenagers surrounded us to enjoy my moves. In amazement, they started asking my cousinMarius, "Where is this man from, who can dance to our music like this?" "He is my cousin," Maruissaid in Lingala, "and he is from London." He told them that I liked Congolese music, and knew the artists better than him as I enjoyed my best evening in the Congo.

It was now time to stay with my cousin, Colonel Youlon, in his hometown of Bacongo. As an experienced senior officer, who had undergone military training in Russia for about five to eight years, it did not make sense that due to 'African politics' he had been sent on 'gardening leave' at home after falling out with the President, Sasso Nguesso. Anyway, as a result I was able to spend another week with him, which was brilliant. He had lost his sister, Mayoma, my dear cousin who died in the plane crash. One day he decided to take me on a tour of Brazzaville. Before he left, just as we were getting into the car, he took out his pistol, and placed it underneath the dashboard. I asked him, "Why are you carrying the pistol?" He replied, "For protection". Straightaway, I became nervous that he might have people, even in the army, who might want to get rid of him because he had fallen out with the President. He took me to the reservoir that supplied the whole of Brazzaville with water. Military men heavily guarded this facility, unlike our country, Sierra Leone, where everywhere is exposed, including strategic areas. That's why when it came to the crunch we were not able to defend the country against invaders from countries like Liberia. We had a very nice day, after all, and went back home safely.

The following week, Mr Gabriel Nzambila took me to Pointe Noire, the second largest city, and main port of the country, with oil companies such as AGIP and ELF engaged in oil exploration in that area. At that time, he acted as assistant director of a mining company in Pointe Noire called Comelog. We flew to Pointe Noire by the National Airline called 'Lina Congo' from Maya-Maya airport, and I felt so proud to be flown by two young Congolese pilots. The flight took about 30-40 minutes across a vast plantation of eucalyptus trees that Mr Nzambila explained was used to make paper. The actual plantations on the ground were vast, producing one of the main exporting products of the Pointe Noire. We collected some cases of fish from the fishing company on the way home, driven by my cousin Henriette. The Nzambilas had a very big, impressive bungalow, and the rest of the family were there waiting to see me. The children present were Fathy, Francis, Mauna and other cousins. A big meal was already prepared, and after about 10-20 minutes rest, we sat round to eat. I wasn't shy because I liked what I saw on the table; it was cassava leaves! The youngest of the children ,Taoma, thought I was shy and kept on saying to me, "Ton ton Sigis," that is "Uncle Sigis."' He was trying to speak English to me. "You eat, you eat." I said to him, "Don't worry, Taoma, I'm eating." This was translated to him in French by his father.

The next day, Sunday, Mr. Nzambila took me on a tour of Point Noire. We started from the port (Matadi) where several ships were busy unloading and loading their cargo, including lots of eucalyptus products. On the way to a village called Diosso, farmers put their products such as firewood, cassava leaves and manioc (that is cassava itself which is used to make foo-foo or to boil and eat with soup on the roadside, reminding me of similar practices at home in Sierra Leone. We also make cassava bread and garri. Whilst in Diosso Mr.

Nzambila took me to a remote place called Diosso Gourges, with a huge crater, covered with a forest. It looked very much like the Grand Canyon, only inhabited by people whom I could hear quite clearly from the distance. In fact, on our way back from Diosso, he took me to some elders, and after the inevitable introductions bought some saca-saca.

I vividly recollect that this was a scary journey during which I started imagining things about lions and other wild animals. What if lions attacked us here? I said to myself. I enquired from Mr. Nzambilla whether there were lions around. He replied in the negative, and asked if I was afraid. I said, "Yes, I don't want lions to come and eat me up; I have to go back to London to join my family." Our next stop was a town called Kouilow. He wanted to show me a bridge, a masterpiece of engineering, and very impressive. On our way back, approaching Diosso, there was a very impressive cemetery with the tomb of a traditional king "Mulango". In the end I very much regretted not taking my camera to record all these wonderful sights. Whilst still in Pointe Noire Mr Nzambila showed me the motor road leading to Gabon and Angola, which seemed very progressive.

On the whole, my trip to Pointe Noire was exciting - a beautiful city, full of wealth and culture. On my last two nights my hosts showed me a bit of the nightlife, and at one of the nightclubs we visited I listened to a very good local band in action. Then my time ran out, and I said some sad farewells, left in the evening for the airport and flew back to Brazzaville. This time I decided to stay with my auntie Beatrice Williams Tamod, and my grandmother Fatoumata. My mother was staying with them. It was Christmas week, and I said, "Thank God I'm going to spend Christmas again in Africa after over twentyyears." In England, people spend and spend, and accumulate debt for that one day. On the actual day itself, you just sit at home watching the Christmas tree, eat, drink, open the presents and talk on the phone. In Africa, it is very lively. People cook big, eat, drink and socialize, with masquerades in the street.

Few days more to go, and before returning I spent most of the time with my grandmother, Fatoumata. We had a good talk, and she told me more about my grandfather, Christopher Williams, her late husband from Sierra Leone, how they'd met, and got married. Valerie Jose, my cousin, speaks English, so she acted as our interpreter. Suddenly, as we were speaking, the music of OK Jazz and Franco, her favourite as well, came on the radio. She got up and started dancing, and seeing her dance, I got up as well and we danced together. Meanwhile friends, and relatives were coming to say bye-bye with gifts for my children, and wife. They knew me well by now so I got lots of LPs and cassettes of the latest Koffi Olomide, Arlus Marbele, Bozi-Boziana, Zaiko Langa-Langa, and Papa Wemba making Congolese music. I could not contain my excitement.

On the day of my departure, I was wondering about my excess luggage. I had paw-paw, pineapples; these were massive and make the ones I see in Peckham market in London look like a joke. For my hand luggage, I had my pineapples and paw-paw in a beautiful woven basket made locally. Before I left Mayama Road in Quenza, Fatoumata spent a few hours with me, and prayed for me. She gave me some chalky substance, which she rubbed on my forehead, and gave me some to bring home to rub occasionally for protection against evil spirits. The next day we left home, the whole family accompanied me to Maya-Maya airport, including my cousin,Henriette, and Mr Nzambila who came all the way from Pointe Noire. Also with them was my cousin, Colonel Youla. We reported at the Aeroflot section of the airport under strict security mainly because of the recent plane crash in which my cousin ,Mayoma, had been killed. My luggage was searched, which was right. The weight was not a problem. Colonel Youla, who was trained at the Russian Military academy, was a friend of the Russian manager. My luggage were given the OK and I was only left with my hand luggage with contents quite visible I was also carrying my large African painting. I had been saved, once again, by 'who knows who.'

It was now time to board. I said farewell to all my friends and relatives who came to see me off. We left Maya-Maya, and in thirty-five minutes, we were in Duala where we stayed for three hours. This time I had time to do some more shopping around the airport. I bought some more arts and crafts. We boarded the plane, and took off for Malta, and then on to London Heathrow.

I arrived home safely to a pleasing welcome from my family. Joan and the girls were most impressed by the size of the pineapples and paw-paw; they were enormous. If they were to sell one of these in Sainsbury or Tesco, one would pay no less than £5 each. I said to my wife, "I'm keeping one of each for my friend, Cleveland Bertram, and his wife Lorraine." He was a colleague at the Brent Careers Service in Wembley. I will never forget my first visit back to Africa after twenty years, and hope I will go back to Congo-Brazzaville one more time before I die because it is a beautiful country, and I had so much fun the first time.

Me, drinking palm wine in a village hut in Bacongo with my nephew standing by

With my nephew on the banks of the River Congo

My mother, 3rd right on her return from Congo, August 1990 with my wife and kids

================= **Chapter 16** =================

My health restored

My medical problems started at the age of about nine or ten years, when I suddenly started having symptoms of swollen ankles, and face. When going to work at the Connaught Hospital in the morning, Dr Marcella Davies would take" me in her car, and see me before anyone else, do the necessary examination, and then give me a prescription to take to the dispensary for medicine. This continued on, and off for a long period causing regular absenteeism from Murray Town Primary School. At the same time, I befriended the young British Army officer in the Sierra Leone Army who came to our shop regularly to do his shopping, and became equally concerned about my illness. He took me to the military hospital at Wilberforce known as "34", but to no avail.

My mother never gave up on me, as she tried everything. We started seeing Pa Shepherd, a popular private dispenser who had his practice at Congo Town, in the premises of Pa Tweede, another popular businessman. She also took me to another private dispenser at Andrew Street, Kroo Town Road, and another one at Circular Road, commonly known as Pa Jeh-Jeh. Finally, Dr Marcella Davies arranged for me to be admitted to Ward One at the Connaught Hospital. In those days they had ten wards and as far as I can remember, if you were admitted in Ward Ten, you were lucky to come out alive. The annex to Ward One was a building known as the Extension. This was the building for the famous and aristocrats in Freetown, the well-to-do's. Staff prepared patients' food in the Extension kitchen, whereas the rest of the other wards patients' food was prepared in an outside kitchen. One could be admitted to Ward One by special arrangement whereby your food would come from the Extension kitchen just as if you were a well-off person admitted in Ward One.

The nurses, and doctors treated me as a favoured young patient, and I remember in particular Dr. Boyle-Hebron, Dr Cummings and of course my own Dr Davies. Some of the nurses who looked after me were Tejan-Cole, Washington, Sangari, Ashley, Nicholls, Nurse Connell, Nurse Addo, and Nurse Williams. My special Nurse was Abdul Sesay. He used to live at Patton Street, and after my discharge from hospital, I would visit him at his house, travelling the long journey from Congo Town in double-decker buses. All of these nurses I have mentioned became leading dispensers, and staff nurses and sisters. One special doctor whom I met during my stay in Ward One, and who I never dreamed of meeting face to face was our future first Prime Minister, Dr. Milton Margai. At that time –pre-independence- he was Chief Minister. It was during that time that I knew he was a medical doctor, although he was beginning to carry the burden of the country. He did find time to make a few visits in the hospitals. He started his rounds, surrounded by some of these top nurses, and Doctor Hebron. They came to my bed and my chart was given to him. He said, "How are you, Mr Tucker?" I replied that I was better, adding, "Sir, I did not suffer from any pain or anything as I can remember, only that my ankles were a bit swollen."

A few weeks later, he made another visit and again, came to my bedside. This time he asked, "How is young Mr Tucker doing?" I replied, "The same." "You take care of yourself," he advised as they moved on. Soon afterwards I left hospital, and everybody said how pleased they were to see me back home. One day a kind gentleman, Pa McCarthy, came to the shop, and told my mother that he would look for a particular "bush medicine" for me; he was a member of the "Congo Town Hunting Society". After a while, he brought with some leaves that looked like sweet potato leaves, only they were broader. As instructed, my mum cooked these leaves, which I enjoyed, and did so on about four occasions. After that I never experienced that kind of illness in again apart from the normal headaches and occasional flu, and that was much later after moving to England.

In 1998, I came to work one day and my colleagues said to me, "Sigi", that's what they all called me, "you are losing weight". I replied, "No I'm on a diet, as my wife told me I ate too much rice. I'm trying to cut down some weight." Some of my colleagues were not convinced, and insisted that my loss of weight could not be due to dieting. I therefore, made an appointment to go and see my GP who took my blood and urine samples for testing. The results showed some sign of kidney failure, and I returned home to break the gloomy news to my wife, and three children. Arrangements were made by my doctor to attend at the Lewisham University Hospital for more tests where my wife, coincidentally, was a Senior Staff Nurse. Lewisham Hospital referred me to Guy's Hospital for more advanced Nuclear Physics test by which time I was getting really worried. As a result, they discovered that I had a small left kidney, the source of my problem. I could not help but reflect that this could have been diagnosed all those many years ago as a young boy growing up in

Sierra Leone, if only we had the proper medical facilities. I still continued working until the day at the Queens Park Community School when I got the phone call from Guys Hospital that I must report urgently. This time all sorts of funny thoughts rushed through my mind. I rang them in the office to inform them. Christmas '98 was approaching. When I reported at Guy's, accompanied by my wife, they took more samples of blood and urine, and then told me the bad news that I had to go on dialysis. I was given lectures on dialysis: there were two types which are haemodialysis, and peritoneal dialysis, the latter of which I had to do myself. I had to undergo training at the Renal Training Centre, St George's Hospital in Tooting for three days, but knew this would not adversely affect me at work especially as I had a very good attendance record so I did not let the illness play on my mind too much.

I went for my training on how to administer the dialysis. Peritoneal dialysis is the liquid form of dialysis which, administered through a tube, goes through your stomach into the peritoneal cavity of the body, where the dialysis is done, removing all waste products. This is the job which is usually done by the kidneys. This whole function had to be carried out under the strictest and cleanest conditions, and I had to do this four times a day, every four hours, the time it took to drain out dialysis liquid. I started this in January 1999 and by the end of September of that year, I suffered three attacks of peritonitis, a severe stomach pain which had to be cured by antibiotics in the hospital. Each time I had the attack, I had to be rushed to Guys Hospital by my son Joe. Around 1:00 a.m. my temperature was very high and the doctor said he would keep me overnight as he could not let me go home with such high temperature. They admitted me immediately, and Joe stayed with me. At this stage I already had my fistula fitted on my left hand for emergency dialysis. This time they had to do some Haemodialysis, this is where the machine does the dialysis on your behalf through tubes connected to your fistula hand. It takes blood to the artificial kidney of the machine which filters it by getting rid of all toxic waste and brings the cleansed blood back into your body. Eventually, I stopped taking peritoneal dialysis. I had to undergo a general operation to remove all tubes from my stomach, and drain myself out properly. In fact on the day of my operation, as I lay recovering in the ward, we had a news flash that there had been a rail crash disaster at Ladbroke Grove in which over 30 people were suspected dead. So I always remember that incident after my operation. A few weeks after recovering, I was immediately sent to Bostock Ward, where the haemodialysis was done. I went for dialysis three nights a week 9.00 p.m.-1.00 a.m., sometimes up to 2.00 a.m. This depended on how quickly I could get on the machine. However, I had a slight advantage from having two Sierra Leonean nursing assistants in this particular ward who were always on night duty. Alice Kargbo and Jenneba Daramy, these assistants, were excellent. They made sure that everything was fine with me. Throughout this period of my dialysis, I reported regularly for work, and no one ever knew that I had a kidney problem unless I told them. But people who knew me realised that I lost much weight whilst remaining fit, though not 100% so.

I remember coming home after having dialysis at 2.30 a.m. Driving home, just as I left Elephant and Castle, heading towards Walworth Road, my Rover car stopped. The engine wouldn't start so I had to call the AA. I waited for over thirty minutes before he arrived. He managed to get me going. As soon as I reached East Dulwich, one of the front tyres punctured. That was about 5.00 a. .m. I parked the car, took the spare from the boot and changed it. I arrived home tired about 6.00 a.m. and went straight to bed;.I rang them at work around 9 00 a.m. to report sick. In May-June 1999, after having my fistula operation, I was told by consultant, James Patterson, that he would put me on the kidney transplant List, which made me very happy as not every kidney patient is fortunate to go on the transplant list for one reason or another.

Meanwhile they asked if any member of my family would be willing to donate a kidney to me because, according to the doctors, a person can live on one kidney. My son, Joe, who was in his final year of his degree course was willing to volunteer, and was invited to meet the transplant sister co-ordinator for counselling on all the necessary tests that were to be taken. In the end, they found out that his kidneys suited me well; tissue type, blood, everything. I told them that they should hold off until his final examination in university before they did the operation. I wanted him to pass his examination. This was an anxious moment for anybody who is on the transplant list; waiting for the day when that phone will ring, whether in your house or office, to hear them say, "You must get ready, for we have got a kidney for you." This was what exactly happened on the 31st January 2001. On this particular day I was in my office in Wembley, not in school where I did most of my work; I was doing the reports we call "Action Plans" in my profession. My colleague, Nana Ali ,walked into my room and sat down to chat with me. This lady cared so much about me during my illness, and always wanted to know what progress was being made about my health. "How are you feeling today?" she asked. "Any news from the hospital?" "I'm feeling fine, but no news yet," I replied. This was about 2.00 p.m. At about 2.30 p.m the phone rang:

"Hello! Sigismond, this is Anne here from Guy's Bostock ward. I've got good news for you. We've got a very nice and suitable kidney from a donor for you. Please come to Guy's immediately."

"OK", I said, "I'll be there soon."

I called Nana. "Guess what," I said. "I've just got a call from Guys; they have got a kidney for me. I have to go." The excitement in me was like someone who had just won the national lottery. I made sure that I completed all my work and handed them to my colleague, Eileen. Everyone wished me good luck as I left the office. I drove very carefully to Brockley where I lived. Being full of excitement, I didn't want this to overcome me, or cause me to have an accident.

I arrived home safely at about 4.00 p.m. My wife was surprised to see me so early.

"Why are you so early today?" she asked.

"I heard good news from the doctor at Guys. They have a kidney for me and I have to report as soon as possible.".

I went upstairs, packed my bag, making sure I had everything. I did not know whether that would be the last I saw of my house and Brockley. I took the bus P3 from my place to London Bridge where Guys Hospital is located. I went to the ward, and reported to Ann who called me with news of the transplant. Doctors came, and did various tests including blood tests. They confirmed that I wouldn't be needing dialysis before the surgery, and transferred me to Richard Bright Ward where a bed was allocated to me. At about 7.00 p.m. the surgeon doing the operation, Professor John Taylor, came and introduced himself, and talked to me about it. He told me about the quality of the kidney on offer, confirming that it was a very good match for me. I became more determined to face the music with confidence. Immediately he left me, two anaesthetists came to my bedside, introduced themselves and explained the role they would be playing in my operation. They then gave me the consent form to sign. As I did so, I thought:Oh God, I'm signing my death warrant." They left. At 11.00 p.m. a nurse and porter wheeled me to theatre and handed me over to the theatre nurse. One of them, a male nurse, introduced himself and said he was from Ghana. I told him I was from Sierra Leone, and instantly there was that African bond between us. "Don't worry," he said, "you are in good hands." The Anaesthetists arrived. I was afraid, seeing all these wonderful big lights and instruments. They said to me, "We are going to put you to sleep." One of them held my right hand and pricked it with some kind of needle. I didn't know what was in it; in a few seconds I lost consciousness. The operation, I was told, took about 5-6 hours. For all I knew at that time, I could have been dead and gone. I knew nothing.

The next morning my wife was at my bedside with all these gadgets attached to my body. I was still drowsy.

The surgeon, John Taylor, was there too. He told me how successful the operation had been, and that I had a good kidney in place. I thanked him, and he left. He visited me several times to make sure I was alright. I then had to fight against organ rejection because somebody else's organ had been transplanted into my body. It's difficult for the immune system to accept a foreign body. I stayed in hospital for about 3-4 months just to make sure that I did not have any rejection. The doctors and nurses worked hard on this, and I was discharged within 4 months of my stay. I'm still attending renal outpatient's clinic. Initially, after my discharge it was three times a week; now it's once a month. At present I feel like a new man. I went back to work six months after my operation. My colleagues were happy that everything had gone well, and thought that I was back to my original self.

Chapter 17

From Diamonds to Nutmeg

I first became interested in Grenada, a lovely island in the Caribbean, since that fateful day at Debenhams when I met a beautiful stranger who would become my wife. I knew nothing about the Caribbean Islands before then, and as I learned more about my spouse's homeland, the setting for the film 'Island in the Sun', starring Harry Belafonte. I became fascinated by the many similarities between her island country and mine, including details like their natural harbour, and turbulent political progress to Independence from the British. It is befitting that I should outline some of these similarities in honour of my wife.

Grenada is an island country, and Commonwealth realm consisting of the island of Grenada, and six smaller islands at the southern end of the Grenadines in the southeastern Caribbean Sea. Grenada is located northwest of Trinidad and Tobago, northeast of Venezuela, and southwest of Saint Vincent and the Grenadines. Its size is 344 square kilometres (133sqmi), with an estimated population of 110,000. Its capital is St George's. The national bird of Grenada is the critically endangered Grenada Dove. Grenada is also known as the 'Island of Spice' because of the production of nutmeg, and mace crops of which Grenada is one of the world's largest exporters. Nutmeg was introduced to the Island in 1843 when a merchant ship called in on its way to England from the East Indies. The ship had a small quantity of nutmeg trees on board which they left in Grenada, and this was the beginning of

Grenada's nutmeg industry that now supplies nearly forty percent of the world's annual crop.

Saint Andrew's is the largest parish in Grenada. The main town is Grenville, which is also Grenada's second largest town after St George's. Marquis was the first Parish Capital from 1795 to 1796, Grenville became capital of Saint Andrew's in 1796. Grenada was first sighted by Europeans in 1498 during the third voyage of Christopher Columbus to the new world. At the time the indigenous Island Caribs (Kalinago), who lived there, called it Camahogne. In 1649, the French founded a permanent settlement on Grenada. Within months this led to conflict with the local islanders which lasted until 1654 when the island was completely subjugated by the French. The French named the new French colony La Grenade, and the economy was initially based on sugar cane and indigo. The French established a capital known as Fort Royal(later St. George). To shelter from hurricanes the French navy would often take refuge in the capital's natural harbour, as no nearby French islands had a natural harbour to compare with that of Fort Royal. The British captured Grenada during the Seven Years War in 1762.Grenada was formally ceded to Britain by the Treaty of Paris in 1763. The French recaptured the Island during the American War of Independence in July 1779. However the island was restored to Britain with the Treaty of Versailles in 1783. On March 1, 1807 the British Parliament passed an Act ending the British Slave Trade. The last British slaver to officially arrive in Grenada was the 'Commerce' of Liverpool that brought 159 Africans from Sierra Leone in February 1808, bringing to an end almost 140 years of that terrible trade. Another vital link between Joan and myself.

In 1950, Eric Gairy founded the Grenada United Labour Party, initially as a trades union, which led the 1951 general strike for better working conditions. This sparked great unrest—so many buildings were set ablaze that the disturbances became known as the 'red sky' days—and the British authorities had to call in military reinforcements to help regain control of the situation. On October 10, 1951, Grenada held its first general elections on the basis of universal adult suffrage - Eric Gairy's Grenada United Labour Party won 6 of the 8 seats contested. On March 3, 1967, Grenada was granted full autonomy over its internal affairs as an Associated State. Herbert Blaize was the first Premier of the Associated State of Grenada from March to August 1967. Sir Eric Matthew Gairy served as Premier from August 1967 until February 1974, and later that year he became the first Prime Minister of an Independent Grenada. Civil conflict gradually broke out between Eric Gairy's government, and some opposition. Gairy's party won elections in 1976, but the opposition did not accept the result, accusing it of fraud. In 1979, the New Jewel Movement (NJM) under Maurice Bishop launched a paramilitary attack on the government resulting in its overthrow. The constitution was suspended and Bishop's 'People's Revolutionary Government' ruled subsequently by decree. Cuban doctors, teachers, and technicians were invited in to help develop health, literacy, and agriculture over the next few years.

Some years later a dispute developed between Bishop and certain high-ranking members of the NJM. Bishop had been taking his time over making Grenada wholly socialist, encouraging private-sector development in an attempt to make the island a popular tourist destination.

Hard line Marxist party members, including Communist Deputy Prime Minister Bernard Coard, deemed Bishop insufficiently revolutionary and demanded that he either step down or enter into a power-sharing arrangement. On October 19, 1983, Bernard Coard and his wife Phyllis, backed by the Grenadian Army, led a coup against the government of Maurice Bishop, and placed Bishop under house arrest. These actions led to street demonstrations in various parts of the island. Bishop had enough support from the population that he was eventually freed after a demonstration in the capital. However, when he attempted to resume power, he was captured and *executed* by soldiers along with seven others, including government cabinet ministers. The Coard regime then put the island under martial law. After the execution of Bishop, the People's Revolutionary Army formed a military government with General Hudson Austin as chairman. The army declared a four-day total curfew, during which (it said) anyone leaving their home without approval would be shot on sight.

Since Joan and I got married I became deeply determined to go and see her parents. So we had to save some money because finances were very tight We just had our son Joe, followed by our daughter Jasmine in 1980. However, we did manage to visit in April 1982. This was a memorable date for us: firstly Grenada was ruled by a revolutionary government headed by the late Prime Minister Maurice Bishop; secondly we were in Grenada when Britain under Prime Minister Margaret Thatcher declared war on Argentina for invading the Falkland Islands. Grenada itself at that time was quiet and peaceful.

We made preparation for our flight to Grenada. We had to travel to London to join the plane from London Heathrow. I knew no one with whom I would be comfortable staying with along with my wife, Joe and Jasmine, except for my good old friend Joe Momoh with whom I was in Bolton, Lancashire. He, and his wife Elsie were very willing to accommodate us for the Saturday to travel on Sunday. He arranged for his friend, Jasper Kemoh, who had a car, to collect us from Euston Station. Little did I know that Jasper Kemoh was going to be my friend. We were staunch members of the SLPP – Sierra Leone People's Party, London, and Ireland branch. I was to become the Assistant Secretary under the Chairmanship of John Saad. Further to that, Jasper Kemoh used to head and run a Training and Employment Centre for which I was to be the Careers Guidance Officer to his students. Six years after meeting him for the first time at Euston Station in 1982, this is what you call "double coincidence".

We had a good time with Joe Momoh on that Saturday before leaving for Grenada on the Sunday. We hired a black taxi cab, driven by a Jamaican man. He entertained us well throughout our journey to Heathrow. We arrived safely and went for check-in. Everything went well and we boarded a BWIA plane. About 7-8 hours later we were in Trinidad, Port-of-Spain Airport. We had to stay there overnight in a beautiful hotel called 'Bel-Air'. There, I had the first taste of Caribbean tropical sun and fresh air, just like my homeland in Sierra Leone after 10-12 years in England. I felt comfortable. To me I felt like I was at home in Sierra Leone.

Early on the Monday we had to take a small plane, 'LIAT', to Grenada because at that time the airport in Grenada could only accept small planes. It took only about forty minutes or so to arrive in Grenada, and the plane was even piloted by a young black man for which I was very proud. I had heard heard so much about my father-in-law, Barclay Celestine alias "Wopa" and mother-in-law, Ethel, sister-in-law Sheila, and brother-in-law, Dominic, "tall boy" as he is known on the island. They all lived in Pierre Marie in Crochu St Andrews. The other brothers - Preston, Augustus and Rupert were all out of the country.

When we arrived in Grenada, Dominic, and Sheila were at the airport waiting for us. They had already hired a big taxi, plus Dominic's car to take us to Crochu, Pierre Marie. This was a hilly area in the country. My first impression of the place was:it looks like Wilberforce in Freetown. We arrived home and we had enough people to take our luggage. Everyone nearby came to see 'Teacher Joan' - that's what they called my wife because she was once a primary school teacher in the village at Crochu Primary School.

Barclay and Ethel were pleased and said, "What we saw from your pictures was not deceiving." We gave out all the presents, and everybody was happy. We felt so happy for the children, especially Joe. Kids were quick to come and befriend them. Soon they were all over the bushes, picking plums and apples. It was nice to see the children playing safely in a natural environment.

My father-in-law "Wopa" was extremely happy to see his daughter, Joan, and myself, and two grand children, Joe and Jasmine. He was an expert at catching local bush meat, a delicacy known locally as "Maniku". The next morning he arrived with two of them, which Ethel used to prepare a delicious soup. Joan liked this, something that she had missed. When the meal was served I couldn't resist the smell; it was delicious! "Wopa" was a very popular man in town. He was a retired carpenter and a very good one. In his days I was told, he was involved in building most of the houses in town. Apart from his main job, he was actively involved in community work, such as helping to construct roads and ringing the gong when someone died in town. He had two donkeys which he used to transport nutmeg to the co-operation in a nearby town called Latante. Further down is another town known as St Davids. This again is another beautiful area with a main former colonial residential area known as Westerhall. It had beautiful houses. There was a playing field nearby, and a cricket match was on. Talking about cricket there were matches everywhere, even in the streets and beaches, you find boys playing cricket. Near our house in Crochu is Felix Park where cricket was also played. I said to myself: no wonder the West Indians are so good at this game.

One day "Wopa" decided to take me around the village. By then he was in his 70s but remained strong and fit. We passed through Felix Park and headed towards a nearby town called Pomme Rose. "Wopa" was showing me off to all his friends. As I watched him, he seemed very happy making the introductions. We came across one of his friends, an old man sitting in his veranda, waiting for the day to go by. As soon as he saw us coming he shouted "Wopa!". The man took my hand and said. "Who is this, Cuban?" At the time there were many Cubans on the island. Anyway, coming back to the old man, he asked "Wopa" if I was Cuban. "Wopa" replied that I was African. The man looked at me in admiration. Within myself, I wondered why he was looking at me like that.

Did I look different? As far as I was concerned, Africans and Caribbeans hade the same roots.

We left Pomme Rose and went down the hill to Latante where he joined his friends in a "rum bar". We only drank soft drinks as both Joan and I do not drink alcohol. People were curious enough to ask which part of Africa I came from, asking me whether I liked Grenada. I replied that of course I liked the place, and if it was left to me I wanted to come and live there now.

I was pleased to actually see the extent of the nutmeg industry, and surprised that there were nutmeg trees everywhere. Nutmeg is one of the main natural resources of the country. Apart from this main crop, the land is blessed, and fertile enough to grow other agricultural products. Traders come with boats from nearby Trinidad to purchase agricultural products, fruits especially. Apart from agriculture, tourism is another main source of income to the country. For a week you may have 4-5 cruise ships. Whilst I was there at the main harbour in St, Georges, I saw the beauty and attractiveness of the country, with a kind of magnetic ingredient in her; you go there once you want to come back.

One day at home I decided that it was my turn to entertain these people in the house. I didn't have much. Luckily for me, my friend in Manchester, Adama Bangura, had just returned from Sierra Leone the week before we left for Grenada. She rang me to say that she brought somecassava leaves. Adama also gave me a bottle of palm oil. I said to myself: these will come in handy.' I decided to take them to Grenada to cook for the family there.There are cassava plants in Grenada, but they don't eat the leaves. The following week after our arrival I was becoming acquainted with the environment. One afternoon we saw "Wopa" coming with this big fish – Grouper, it was. "I brought this for you so that Ethel will cook nice soup and dumpling for you," he said. I cut the fish in two halves and took the tail end of it and smoked it dry. It was perfect just as we do in Sierra Leone because you can't cook cassava leaves with raw fish; it has to be smoked. Whilst I was doing this, Ethel was watching me. She said to Joan, "What is he doing?" Joan replied, "Wait and see." Next day, I got everything ready to do the cooking. Joan was with me. I had boiled the meat earlier and everything was finished in an hour. As the saying goes, "The proof of the pudding lies in the eating." We all sat down to eat. I had some nice African tapes - Congolese, of course: Orchestre Veve and Sosoliso. These were two great bands from the Congo. The food was good, they said, and the music was electric; put shocks on their feet and got everyone moving. Some went for more food. They'd never eaten anything like this before nor heard such music. I got up and displayed a few steps of rhumba.

Time to return to England was around the corner. We were sad to leave. After this visit my wife and children went back to Grenada many times whilst I went to Congo-Brazzaville, followed by a visit to my country, Sierra Leone in 1990/91 for the first time in twenty years; I was glad to be back especially to see my old friends, and family.

In January 2002, we lost "Wopa". A few months after I left Grenada in 1982, he was given an award by the Government for community work - an award that was well deserved. He died of old age at ninety-three, peacefully, in his sleep. Unfortunately, I couldn't go for the funeral in Crochu, but I was told it was attended by over a thousand mourners. The local St Martin's church was full beyond capacity. I spoke to my mother-in-law, Ethel, and apologised for not coming and promised her that I would come for the memorial service in January 2003.

At the end of January 2003 Joan left for Grenada. I left on the 9th. We both managed to travel by Monarch Airlines, which goes direct to Grenada and then on to Tobago. The first thing that caught my eye on arrival was the beauty of the new airport, small but beautiful and well organised. Everything was orderly. No-one is expecting you to "put for me" - in Sierra Leone parlance, "give me a bribe" before you can go through. This can cause lots of embarrassment to people. I went through customs with no hassle; Joan and Dominic were waiting for me at the Aarrivals. Coming out of the airport, I began to see developments from what I left twenty years ago; beautiful buildings, good roads, street lights, telephone boxes everywhere, and lots of business enterprises. Dominic then drove me to the medical school of the University of West Indies. The campus was first class, more than some I've even seen in England. It was a long drive from St Georges up to Crochu in St Andrews, but we eventually arrived safely. Mummy, the name I call Joan's mother, Ethel, was very happy to see me. I could see the relief on her face to see that I was back to my normal self after a recent illness. We rested for a while and then we had a nice soup with dumplings which she prepared. I knew something Caribbean was waiting for me and I made sure I "dealt" with it properly. One thing I missed was the mango. On my first trip I ate nearly half a bucket of "common mango", as we call it in Sierra Leone. In the Caribbean they call it "Julie Mango", very sweet. Anyway, this time mango was out of season, as the trees were just beginning to flower.

On my second day I was anxious to visit downtown Grenville, just out of curiosity to go and see the changes. Dominic had a jeep and on our way we went through Hope City. This is a nice area with lovely buildings. We eventually arrived in Grenville. This is a town located by the sea front, very commercial, with the port authority there as well. Boats arrived with container goods and fisherman also arrived with their catches. At one of the shops we visited, to my amazement, the young lady who served us caught my raw African accent. She said to me in the presence of Joan, "Excuse me are you from Africa?" "Yes", I replied. "You sound as if you are from Sierra Leone." "I am," I replied. "Me sef na Salone are komot", she said in krio, meaning, "I'm from Sierra Leone too." "Oos part na Salone you komot?" I asked her ("What part of Sierra Leone are you from?") "Are komot Kroo Town Road," she replied, meaning, "I'm from Kroo Town Road." This is very commercial area in Freetown with all the Indian and Sri-Lankan traders. "Na Lebanese School ar go", meaning, "I attended Lebanese School" This is one of the most expensive private schools in Freetown. I told her that my sister, Emelia Balasubramaniam, has two daughters who attended that school. She was amazed at my sister's last name, so I explained to her that her husband was from Sri Lanka. My wife Joan was just amazed to hear us conversing in Krio. She just uttered the words, "What a small world." And we were lucky; we got a huge discount that day, and everybody was happy!

"Joan and Dominic," I shouted, "let's go to the fish market". "I like fish", I said. As soon as we went the fishermen were arriving with their catch. There were lots of big fishes, particularly one big one they called "king fish". It caught my eye and I suggested to Dominic that we got one for mummy. We went for it and it was Ec75.00 dollars. They cleaned and cut it into pieces; great fish, and very delicious to eat. It was the big day on my first Sunday. The memorial service for Barclay Celestine "Wopa", was at the village Roman Catholic Church, St Martins, with a beautiful big mural at the back of the altar, depicting Jesus meeting John the Baptist by the river Jordan and the dove descending from Heaven. In fact, the theme for the sermon on that Sunday was 'baptism'. Special prayers were said for "Wopa" and other bereaved families. Immediately after the service we went to the late man's graveside: Joan, Ethel, Dominic and I - just as we do in Africa, to talk to the dead. We call it libation. I shouted by the graveside, "Wopa" it's me Sigi. I have come all the way from London to talk to you. I know you are in God's hands; look after us and protect the family." We spent some 20-30 minutes with "Wopa" and went home.

The following Wednesday we had a prayer meeting in the house for "Wopa" and the rest of all the relatives who had died recently, including Neil, commonly known as "Flash". He died suddenly after "Wopa" in Easter 2001. This was the "right hand man" of my brother-in-law Dominic. In preparation for this prayer meeting we went to Grenville to do some more shopping. It was a big prayer meeting. Female elders of the church came and conducted the meeting. Rupert, my other brother-in-law and his friend,were there, drinks flowing from left and right. I had managed to buy a few bottles of hard drinks from a Peckham supermarket "Lidl" which I had brought along. The house was full of ladies. By this time a neighbour called Glenda, whom Joan taught in school, had finished making the fish cakes and sliced bread to serve to guests after prayers.

It started at about 8.30pm. I had never in my life witnessed such a long prayer meeting. Rupert's friend, who earlier was talking about how good he was in catching and cooking maniku and armadillo, got involved in the prayers, and singing as well. To everyone's amazement he could recite every word of these prayers, and knew all the hymns. He was an interesting character. Sometimes when people feel that they are nobody in society I always befriend them and listen to what they have to say. Halfway through the prayers he was already drunk. He drank lots of rum and whiskey earlier and fell asleep. Prayers were not coming from him anymore.

Suddenly, there was a voice towards the end of the prayers. It was Dominic's. "Say prayers for "Flash"," he said. One of the old women asked what his real name was. "Neil", he replied. Everyone in town knew him as "Flash". The women started to pray for Neil more than five times. Dominic was pleased. "Flash's" death affected him greatly. He still hasn't recovered from his friend's death. Worst of all, it was 7.00 a.m. one morning, two days before our departure, we heard the phone ringing. Mummy picked it up. It was Rupert. He immediately told Mummy that he had had this dream last night in which "Flash" appeared to him and told him that somebody poisoned him. When Mummy told us this, Dominic replied that he had been suspecting all along that "Flash's" death was not an ordinary death. Now the cause of his death had been revealed in a dream.

"Tomorrow we go round the island", Dominic said. I was happy, and looked forward to that. He was a good driver, brilliant mechanic, and possessed two Cherokee jeeps. We were safe. We took off from Crochu, came down to Grenville and went round all the other parishes: St Patrick, St Marks, Victoria, and "Gouave, the town that never sleeps", as Dominic put it. But one memorable and historic scene we visited was a town called Sauteurs. We went to the cemetery on top of a hill, surrounded by deep sea. Just by the edge where there was a steep slope, with a sign saying "Caribs' Leap". This was the place where Caribs leaped into the sea rather than surrender to the French who were after them with guns and cannons, the usual "trade mark" of colonialism in those days.

Grenada is surrounded by the beautiful sea. For us in Crochu, we had our own local beach called Cabea. "Let's go for a dip" he said; that's swimming. He likes swimming. Not a single day goes by without him going for a dip, in fact, he carries swimming trunks and a towel in his jeep, so wherever he is and when he feels like having a dip he will.

St Georges Harbour, Gran Anse, Hope or Cabea you name it, he will have a dip. When it comes to swimming I'm completely useless, which is a shame because coming from Murray Town in Freetown which is almost surrounded by water most people I grew up with, boys and girls can swim. For me the real reason I can't swim is because as a young boy growing up in Murray Town, I almost drowned at a local place called "Banana Wata". I went to dive for fish, after one of the local fishermen had blasted some mullets with dynamite; it was, "Borbor Acara" (his nickname) He was my friend from "Cole Farm", Murray Town. Lots of mullets floated and I went to the deep end where I almost drowned, but I managed to fight my way out. Since then I'm always scared to go out in the deep. This fright was intensified when in Grenada we went to a beach called "Bathways". This is a popular beach for family days out. I was told before we arrived that this was a place with natural barrier dividing the sea, and pool where people swam. Beyond the divide you would either drown, or get eaten by sharks. Even Dominic, who is a very good swimmer, never crossed the divide. It's frightening! As for me, I never stepped into that particular stretch of water. Joan found this most amusing, and could not stop laughing at me!

Our days in Grenada were coming to an end. All we were thinking about was returning to the cold. I didn't want to come back to England for I loved Grenada. I was very impressed with the rate of development, the Prime Minister, Dr. Keith Mitchell and his team, a young and dynamic leader with a good sense of direction. I miss my "roti" and "lambi" and more especially the two dogs, Flora and Brownie, who had taken to me during my two-week stay. They would follow me all the way from Pierre Marie down to Crochu Junction. One last errand I had to fulfil and that was to collect nutmegs because I had promised my Aunty Babs in Manchester that I would bring back some nutmegs and cinnamon for her. She likes to make lovely cakes. I thought to myself: Grenada, by the grace of God I'm coming back. I hope you will adopt me as your son.

My wife Joan and I at Caribs' Leap

Island of Grenada

Nutmeg

======== **Chapter 18** ========

Going back to Freetown after the war

In 2004 around Easter, I decided to take my wife and three children to see this wonderful country I'd been telling them about. I warned them beforehand what they should expect to see – a damaged country, destroyed by irresponsible politicians, helped by brutal and unpatriotic soldiers, and worst of all, Charles Taylor and his collaborators, the rebels.

My family were nervous of me taking them because of the bad images they had been seeing on television - all the atrocities that had been taking place during this period. On the day of the Johnny Paul military coup that overthrew President Tejan Kabba, my cousin, Madame Rosalie Tamod Monthault was in Freetown visiting my mother, and family. She was a Congolese Diplomat based in Paris. She stayed with my sister, Emelia, at Aberdeen Ferry Road.

I had earlier arranged with Mrs Patricia Kabba (nee Tucker) late wife of the President, for them to meet. I spoke to her frequently at the Presidential Lodge, and they were to meet on the Tuesday after the Sunday coup. That's a day I'll never forget because we were in Walworth Road Methodist Church for a thanksgiving service for our Collegiate School Old Boys Association, England Branch, when we heard of the coup. My mind was wandering, thinking of all kinds of images because the soldiers were behaving like savages ; no discipline, occupying people's houses, looting, commandeering people's vehicles and so on. The lawabiding citizens in the country went through hell. Luckily, foreign diplomats were airlifted by helicopter to neighbouring Guinea (Rosalie told me later when I visited her in Paris). She told me of horrors she saw and how she managed to get back to Paris. Of course she never saw Mrs. Kabba; they themselves had to flee to Guinea where they took refuge.

With all these in my mind it was a big gamble taking my family there. I persuaded them to come, assuring them that peace had returned to the country.

Two months before our departure I shipped a barrel of groceries and a trunk, through my friend, and school mate who ran a shipping business. He assured me that they would be safe on arrival in Freetown's port. That was not to be; upon arrival in Freetown, the trunk was damaged, and some of my things pilfered. This was the second time this had happened to personal effects I shipped to Freetown. I also bought our flight tickets through my friend, the shipper. The flight was the so-called Sierra National Airlines (SNA). Up till that time, Sierra Leone could not boast of a national airline; what they had then, flying as Sierra National Airlines, was a leased plane belonging to Iceland. Since independence our country has not been able to run our airlines properly without leasing and even at this they always ran into problems with the contracts.

We arrived at Gatwick on the day of the flight. I heard so many stories about SNA at Gatwick – flight delays, harassment for luggage etc. I had it in my mind that I was not going to let anyone harass me, or my family. On that day so many people were going to Sierra Leone, some coming from America on connection. The queue was long and seemed never-ending. For me, being very time-conscious, I made sure we arrived early to get good positions on the queue. Some people had a rough time checking in, but I think they saw it on my face that I was not in the mood to accept any nonsense.

We boarded the plane and, to be honest, the flight was quite good. I was a bit disappointed when, halfway through the flight, the captain announced that we were going to land at Banjul in the Gambia. We had been told it was going to be a direct flight, so I said to one of the air hostesses, "What kind of nonsense is this? I thought it was a direct flight?" She apologised and that was all, we had no choice. I was glad when we arrived in Banjul because, at least, we were on African soil. For me it had been thirteen years since I last visited Freetown, but for my family it was the first time coming to Africa. Through the windows we saw all the planes at the airport. We took off for Freetown. I knew it would be under an hour. I said to my family we are going to be in Freetown soon. All the time I was thanking God we were going to arrive safely.

In no time at all, the Captain announced that we were about to land at Lungi Airport, the only international airport in Sierra Leone, far away from Freetown across the estuary of the River Rokel. I was not expecting a very good airport after the war, but to our surprise it was nice. My sister, Emelia, was there waiting. Again, I had heard a few frightful stories about this airport, like having to be careful to whom you gave your luggage to handle as so many porters offered to help, with the expectation of good tips. I managed to get through Customs with a few tips to the officers. Then you should have seen the number of porters that rushed through to assist us. Emelia just shouted at them not to touch the luggage. She had already arranged her own porters to help us. I gave her £5 notes for the two of them.

We boarded a coach which I thought was going to take us to the ferry terminal; instead it took us to the hovercraft terminal. There was a bar with some nice reggae music blasting all the time. My wife liked it. About 12.00 a.m. we spotted the lights of the hovercraft coming from a far distance. Suddenly it was landing by the beach. That looked impressive! Joan and the children were excited, so was I. Within thirty minutes after unloading and loading of luggage, we were onboard. It was a very enjoyable ride, and everything went well, without any hiccups. I have always been afraid of the ocean, and all along the journey, I prayed for our safety, and God answered my prayer. We arrived at the Aberdeen terminal at about 1.00 a.m. I spotted my sister, Olor, and her husband, Mr. Swarray, and their daughter Adama. A Pajero 4-wheel drive vehicle was waiting, and in no time we were home in Byrne Lane. We stayed at my sister, Emilia's. My mother was there waiting for us. She lives just next door. We chatted until about 3.00 a.m. By that time everyone was tired. We got up very late, and sat on the veranda where we had complete view of both the Aberdeen River and Aberdeen Village on the other side. Aberdeen is, perhaps, the main entertainment centre onn the outskirts of Freetown.

Joan was quick to take up the phone to ring her mum in Grenada in the Caribbean. She was excited to say to her mum, "I'm in Africa.Freetown looks just like Grenada." This confirmed what I had been telling her for a long time!

On our first day I decided to take them just to the neighbourhood to see one, or two old friends. The first person we visited was Mrs. Beatrice George-Pratt. She had met Joan, and the children in England on a visit to her daughter, Dr. Ekundayo George-Pratt. I had told my family that I lived with them before coming to England. We saw a few more neighbours, including Moses Lewis, the grandson of Sir Samuel Lewis, the first Sierra Leonean to be knighted. As soon as he spotted me, he became very excited, ran towards me, shouting my name with joy. The reason he was shouting so loudly was because he had become deaf over the years. I introduced him to my wife, and family. He looked at my boy and asked him, "Do you keep goal like your dad?" He demonstrated to him how I used to catch and dive for balls, "Not like Amadu Kargbo." (the number one goalkeeper for Sierra Leone in those days, but I had not been too far from him, though not as passionate like him. He was a professional.

Day two of my visit was to take them around town. I was determined to see certain people who were very helpful to me when I was in Sierra Leone. One of them was my friend, retired Judge Donald Macaulay. He meant everything to me. I brought some nice presents for him. How was I to locate him? I went to the Law Courts building, my old place of work, by the historic Cotton Tree. Some members of staff did recognise me: Victor Horton, now a senior administrator, Mr Fowler and Shirley Coker were still there. Mildred Solomon (nee Cole) was not in the office. I enquired from Victor where I could locate Donald Macaulay. We came out of the building, and stood by the National Petroleum Station to look at the historic Cotton Tree which has been a national heritage of the country for over two centuries.

They were admiring the thousands of bats hanging from the branches. My daughter, Jean Marie, was busy video-taping. We then took a stroll further down, and came to Wilberforce Street where Donald's office is. Mr Fowler introduced me to the secretary but unfortunately Donald had gone to lunch. I left the gifts, and my complimentary card. She told me he would be back between 2.00 and 3.00 p.m. I left a message with her for him to wait for me.

Meanwhile, we took a walk to Walpole Street to see my other good friend Arnold Gooding, also a prominent barrister and solicitor. We went to his office, and the secretary let him know I was around with my family from London. He immediately came out and took us to his chambers to give us a warm welcome. I introduced my family to him. We were there for almost an hour. He told us about the horrors of the war. Unfortunately we came at a bad time, for he was travelling to London the next day, otherwise he would have invited us for dinner in his house. We were glad to see each other, and parted company. I am not sure when I'll see him again.

Freetown was very hot. I'm sure the temperature was about 80-85 degrees Fahrenheit. My wife said it was hotter than Grenada, but I said otherwise. There followed a short argument about which country was hotter. After that I decided to take them to King Jimmy Market by the river front in central Freetown. I also showed them the main hospital and the nurse's training school, not far from the market, which was of interest to her as a senior staff nurse herself. By this time, I could see the tiredness in their faces, so I decided to stop a taxi to take us to Donald, as it was now 2.30 p.m. This time he was there, expecting us. We embraced each other, and sat down in a semi-circle round his massive desk. He looked very well, and affluent, more than when I left him.

I introduced my wife Joan, my son Joe at that time an Executive Officer in the Inland Revenue, my daughter Jean-Marie Aminata, and Adama my niece. He asked his staff to bring in some cold drinks. First, he thanked me for the lovely present I brought for him, and said how much he appreciated it. He, too, told me about the horrors of the war. When I asked him how he managed to survive, he replied, "Well, Mr Tucker, by the Grace of God we survived." My wife spoke about the Caribbean and the children spoke about themselves. We went on and on, then suddenly he asked us what plans we had for the next day evening. We replied that we did not have anything planned. He then promised to send his driver to pick us up to have dinner with his family. I gave him the directions to where we lived, at Byrne Lane.

The next day, his driver arrived at exactly 7 p.m. in a Mercedes Benz vehicle to pick us up. He took us, including Adama, to join him, his son Don-Martin, and partner Jenny. We met them at the Cape Light-House Club in Aberdeen Village. That was the best evening I've ever had in my country, and he made me proud to be in my country with my family who were complete strangers. We were there for over 3 hours, having all kinds of delicious food, and drinks. My stomach was "whispering" to me, "don't take anymore". About 1 am he took us across the road to his casino. That was another memorable experience. We all had a gamble that night with Joe wining Le 50,000! It was great fun. We parted company, and the driver took us back to Byrne Lane.

Day four - it was my day to take them around my former "territory". Firstly, I had to show them Collegiate School, which is just round the corner from Byrne Lane. I brought six footballs and a pump, the latest fashion from a sports shop in Wembley which Joe presented to the staff and some pupils who were around. We took a group photograph. Suddenly, the Principal Nathaniel Davies, my classmate arrived. He recognised me immediately, and we embraced each other. He then showed his staff our football team portrait in his office. That picture was taken after we won the school's championship. Staff in the picture included Mr M.A. Garber, vice Principal Victor Hastings-Spaine, and Games Master M.S. Turay, a great guy. He pointed to them: "You see him, that's him there (referring to me) and he was one of the goalkeepers for "Mighty Blackpool". Mighty Blackpool was one of the leading football clubs in the country. I was very proud of myself at that moment. This sort of reinforced all what I had been telling Joe, and his mother about my teenage days. Nathaniel took us round the school to show me what needed to be done, and what support they would require from the Old Boys Association in the U.K. I took pictures and told him I would report back to the Association in the UK.

Our next destination that day was to take them to the main town, the popular Murray Town. Before that we went back to the house to take gifts for my friend, Mama Ade Dixon, former village post mistress. All these years she had been pleading with me to bring my family on holidays to Sierra Leone. She wanted to see my wife, especially as she had told me repeatedly that I had a very beautiful wife. I had been promising her that one day she would see her. The irony was that she went blind a few years before our arrival., so the day that I took my wife, and children she couldn't actually see them. We spent over an hour with her, causing her to shed a few tears about the past. Nonetheless, I left her very happy. Opposite Mama Ade's house was my friend Sam Walker's dad's house. We crossed the road and saw the great man himself. Of course, he couldn't recognise me anymore until I said "Humble, Mama Janet's son." Suddenly all the excitement began to build up. Again we stayed for an hour and left him happy before we departed.

Still in Murray Town I showed them Mummy's house in Milton Street, then took them to the school yard, and the church I attended (Ebenezer Methodist) whilst we were living in this village.

By this time, Good Friday and Easter Sunday were fast approaching. My mother planned to slaughter three pigs to sell to neighbours, and to keep some of the best portions to cook whilst we were there. The morning of the slaughtering I thought I should wake up to help. I invited Joan, and the children to come and watch, but they could not bear the sight. Fumi, my nephew, and "Sorie Munku" were the main butchers. "Sorie Munku" was socalled because he was a bit of a fool. In our youth, he used to spend his money on going to Roxy and Odeon cinemas to watch cowboy films. All he talked about was the fastest in the west - John Wayne, Roy Rogers, and Franco Nero. He was an interesting character, though - the same old "Sorie Munku". I liked him.

Easter Sunday: I persuaded my wife we should attend Hephzibar Church. It, was undergoing some reconstruction, and refurbishment but they managed to hold services, regardless. The Easter service was well attended and was conducted nicely. They asked my wife to be the receiver which she did with pleasure, but Joan felt a bit embarrassed when one of the Church wardens announced her, and remarked, "Is she not beautiful?" and the congregation replied, "Very" and applauded. At this stage I made a brief introduction of myself, and informed them that I wa a founder member of this church and reminded them how we used to hold services in the early days:under the shade of the trees. And I told them my wife was from the Caribbean island of Grenada. It proved a very good Sunday for our family, and a memory I'll always cherish.

Behind this happiness of visiting my country once more after the war there was sadness too. A friend I grew up with in Byrne Lane had been brutally killed by the ECOMOG soldiers when they came to Freetown to get rid of Johnny Paul Koroma, the leader of the junta running the government, and his close allies, the rebel fighters. If they were soldiers enough they should have stayed and put up a fight instead of running away to the bush. They didn't have the guts to fight proper soldiers.

Rumour had it that my friend had had some kind of affiliation with Johnny Paul, and as such was one of the people the ECOMOG soldiers were looking for. I was told that the Nigerian ECOMOG Commander was a no-nonsense man. They picked up my friend, took him down to the river, and shot him.His body was found a few days later. I wouldn't like to wish such a tragic death on anybody. May His Soul Rest In Peace!

We did have a pleasant few weeks in Freetown. My, wife and children enjoyed touring parts of Freetown. Emelia hired a taxi for us during our stay which took us everywhere, including the university, Fourah Bay College, and a on trip around the peninsula.

Before our departure, I went to say goodbye to my friend, Donald Macaulay. All of us went again to his office, and there was a surprise gift waiting for us. It was a fine local wood carving , what you would call a masterpiece: Moses receiving the Ten Commandments from God. From the moment I received it, I began to ponder how I would get it through Lungi Airport without harassment.

I had had to re-book our flight three days before our departure. We were told that we were leaving Saturday evening, arriving at Gatwick on Sunday morning. We joined the Hovercraft once again from Aberdeen Terminal for Lungi Airport, with Emelia accompanying us. We arrived safely after a good ride across a calm river.

We did all the check-ins, after jumping several hurdles which required lots of tips. My last hurdle was going through with my carving because it was large, and I had wrapped it in a piece of cloth for protection. The officer couldn't take his eyes off it for it was a magnificent piece of work.

"What is this?" he said.

"What do you think it is?" I replied.

"You are to pay customs for this."

"It is a gift," I replied, "from my friend Donald Macaulay, I didn't buy it.".
"You mean Donald Macaulay the retired Judge?"

"Yes" I replied. "Ok, go with it."

"Thank you, I replied.

We boarded the plane around 10.00 p.m. and took off, bound for London. We had a smooth flight through the night, and arrived London Gatwick at 6.00 a.m. One week after arrival I put in an insurance claim for cancellation of flight. The Norwich Union asked me to get a letter from the Sierra National Airlines to confirm the cancellation of the flight, which I did through the ticket agency. Believe you me; I'm still waiting for a reply! Maybe I should have chased it, so I will never know if they received it.

Joan my wife, Adama my niece and my daughter Jean-Marie, and son Joe at Liverpool street in Freetown after coming from Connaught Hospital.

Coming towards Rawdon Street,in Freetown,Joe leading the Troupe.

The Historic Maroon Church, located at Siaka Stevens Street in Freetown

Mother Janet at her residence in Byrne Lane, Aberdeen Ferry Road

==================== **Epilogue** ====================

In memory of our loving son, Joe

Just as I was about to send my book for publication, tragedy struck in my family. Without any warning, my son Joseph Abioseh Dominic Tucker died in his sleep in his flat in Manchester. Joe had no record of any medical condition since birth, apart from the usual flu or headache once in a while. He went to work on the 26th February 2009 and on the morning of Friday the 27th he reported to the director of his team for Tax Data Securities that he was not feeling very well. He was told to have a rest for that day and that if it got worse he would send a doctor round. Joe never had the chance to ring his mother or myself to say how he was feeling or even any of the good friends I had introduced him to in Manchester: Mr. Joe Renner, his godfather, Mr. Theodore Johnson, or his best friend from childhood, Lee Gray. These were people with whom he exchanged visits regularly. His Director was the last to speak to him. Joe went to bed and died in his sleep.

He moved to Manchester in July, 2007 to his new post as part of a team working for H.M. Revenue and Customs. Prior to that appointment he was the staff manager of H.M. Revenue and Customs in London's Blackfriars branch at 28 when he first started with Inland Revenue. He worked as a Collectors' Executive in 2004.

Who was this remarkable young man? Born in Fallowfield, Manchester on the 10th July, 1977, at the age of three, we noticed he was something special. We thought he was going to be very athletic because being my first child and very proud of him, I used to carry him on my shoulder. I was probably a bit of show-off about my " boy-son", as we say in Freetown. I would carry him from West Didsbury, Manchester, until we arrived at the junction of Wilmslow Road and Ladybarn Road where I knew the traffic is safe. I would put him down and then the running began He would run from Ladybarn Road to Brailsford Road. Obviously his mother enjoyed his athleticism. That's when we said to each other, "This boy is going to be an athlete." But he never was. Instead he played five-a-side football for his Inland Revenue side at the Kennington Playing Park in London, Camberwell New Road, Kennington.

Joe attended Mauldeth Road primary school in Manchester, and as a toddler he was always curious to find out how things worked, especially his toys. He would dismantle them and fix them again in working order. He grew up with this ability until he was ready to attend secondary school. He was just eleven when I got a job with the

London Borough of Brent and I started working for the Education Careers Service. Joe was down in time to start his secondary education with St Thomas the Apostle School in Nunhead. Throughout his primary and secondary education, he never gave us any cause to attend any form of disciplinary hearing. He was not a particularly clever boy but he had enough intelligence to get him through in his short life.

He completed his secondary education with reasonable GCSE passes which enabled him to get a 6th form place in St Francis Xavier in Clapham. He finished classes late because he had to do maths, in which he had a D grade, to improve it to B or C, so that every day, I had to go and pick him up late in the evening. With the gun and knife culture sweeping Britain's young people I didn't want anyone to hurt or bully my son. At St Francis he did BTEC National Diploma in Business Administration and IT for 2 years. He completed that and gained admission to Westminster University to do an H.N.D. (Higher National Diploma) in Administration and Information Technology. Again he completed it (a two- year course) successfully and applied to South Bank University where he gained entry to the 2nd year B.A. (Hons) degree course in Administration and Information Technology. Whilst studying he did part-time work with Sainsbury supermarket in New Cross. Upon completion of his degree course he was transferred from the shop floor as Assistant to the Administration when he was made a member of the Price Control team. Whilst working in this position, Joe saw an advertisement for the Civil Service Executive examination and decided to take it. He was successful on the first attempt, was invited for an interview, was successful in that one and was invited for a second interview at which he was also successful. He was appointed and was sent to work with the Inland Revenue Elephant & Castle in 2004. In 2006 he was appointed as staff manager with the merged H.M. Revenue & Customs in London Blackfriars branch. He was in this position until July 2007 when he moved to Manchester, his home town, which he loved so much. To crown it further, the grounds of Manchester United, the football club he idolised was just nearby.

On Sunday 1 March 2009, United won the Carling Cup Final around 7.00 p.m. We thought we should ring him to congratulate him and discuss the match. We rang him on his mobile, and got no reply, and he never came back to us; usually when you left a message on his mobile or home phone he would come back within minutes. We kept on ringing with no reply. I was getting worried. I suggested to the rest of the family that maybe he had lost his mobile, which sometimes came out of his pocket and fell in the corner of the settee. It took some time for him to find it. My wife continued to ring at intervals until 1.00 a.m,,still no reply.

Monday the 2nd March, I continued to ring. However I left for work. We lived in Brockley and my office, Prospects Ltd Connexions Centre was in Southwark - Rye Lane Peckham. The phone calls continued but with Joe not answering. Around 10.00 a.m. my wife decided to ring his office to find out if he had gone to work. A member of the team answered and said he is not there as yet. "This is unusual for Joe," Joan said, "because he is always one of the first to get to the office." Two colleagues accompanied by a policeman went to his flat and found Joe dead in his bed. By the time my friend, Joe Renner, arrived at his flat he saw it cordoned off by the police and an ambulance removing the body. A few minutes later, I got a call from the police. The caller said, "Mr Tucker, this is the police here. I'm sorry to say that we've found your son, Joe, dead in his flat." That was horrible news for me. I ran to our office canteen, crying. Colleagues came to me trying to console me. As I wept, I just kept on saying, "My beautiful boy is dead". My colleague, Desiree, decided to take me home, to find another crying session: my wife and two girls.

That evening we went straight to Euston and booked an open ticket to Manchester. We couldn't stay with my sister Beatrice because she was on holidays in Freetown and so we had to stay with Joe's Uncle Ces. For the next few days we stayed with him in Farnworth. Luckily Uncle Ces and wife Pam were both on holidays so we were quite comfortable with them. We had an appointment with the Coroner Liaison Officer in Salford who told us what' was going to happen when someone was found dead in such circumstances. First, he said, there was going to be a post mortem and we would be invited to go and identify Joe in the mortuary. On Wednesday, 4th April, accompanied by Ces and Pam together with Joe's childhood and faithful friend, Lee Gray, we went to Salford General Hospital Mortuary where the coroner was expecting us. We were taken to the room where they laid Joe. He looked very clean and healthy and strong as usual, just sleeping peacefully forever. I played with him, kissed him, so did everyone else. Joe couldn't wake up. After we identified him the coroner took us to a room to interview and take statements from us.

Midway through taking the statements and Joe's profile he said to us, "What a fine young and progressing man." Everyone in the room said, "Yes, he was," and the tears started pouring out from all present. We could even see signs of sadness from the coroner as if he was saying to himself: what a waste. For us, we believe that Joe was on a mission to this planet Earth; he came, he saw and he conquered – mission accomplished. God gave him to us and took him back. He made everyone happy during his short life - even those with whom he interacted either at work or socially.

Three weeks after his burial, a West Indian lady with whom I travel to work on the bus every morning greeted me with, "How are you this morning?"

"Not too good," I replied.

"What's the matter?"

"I just buried my thirty-one- year-old son."

"Oh, I'm very sorry to hear about that," she said. She felt as sorry as if she was part of my family. Two weeks later we met once more and she said to me,

"I've been thinking about your son. I wonder if he was the young man I saw you with, standing at the bus stop carrying a bag?"

"Yes," I replied, "he was; that's Joe alright. We always went to Peckham on a Saturday whenever he was down from Manchester."

"I used to see him every morning when he was living over there in one of those new flats," she said,That's over David Rowcastle Road, named after the Late David Rowcastle the famous Arsenal and England footballer who was also living nearby in Brockley. "He was such a nice handsome man, very polite, well dressed and always said hello to me when we met at the bus stop. I said to her, "That's him alright". I could see tears coming from her eyes which also made me shed some tears. We said goodbye to each other and parted company.

Annex to the Epilogue

What follows now are the many tributes coming from work colleagues from various H.M. Revenue and Customs, and their Chief Executive from Whitehall in Parliament Street. The many tributes speak for themselves what kind of promising and useful citizen we produced in England, a real role model for black young men, the one of many you hardly see on British television if you're not a sports man or in show business.

Joe lives on forever in our lives only we can't see him. Now I don't have someone to fix the video, DVD player or television. Nor even to mend his sister's computers when there is a virus – doing these things were as easy as ABC to Joe.

"Joe, we miss you very much and we love you forever, may you rest in perfect peace ...."

Tributes

From: Sissy, Grandmother in Sierra Leone

Please accept my sympathy for the death of Joe Joe. What a great loss that has come upon us. The only son, better if had me been die but you both should buck up. I mourn for my Joe, Joe that I don't even watch television. I'll wait until burial is over before I watch television. Amble, buck up do I beg you it is the will of god.

Joseph Tucker Forever Young – by his family

Why God chose to take Joe so soon, we will never fully understand. But Heavenly Father, we thank you. Thank you for blessing us with the wonderful life of our Joe. It was short, but how very sweet it was.

We feel that Joe was sent here on a mission, an angel here on earth whose goal it was to bring people together and spread a little happiness. He radiated positivity, jokes were always aplenty and his kindness, cool and gentle demeanour touched many people's hearts. Those who either knew Joe for many years, briefly met him or did not have the opportunity to meet him, knew what a uniquely special man he was.

Joe loved nothing more than to be with his family and close network of friends. To Joe, no night out on the town could compare to being at home with his family (although he was starting to enjoy the Manchester nightlife!)

Joe's life story began and ended in his beloved city of Manchester. To say Joe had a very happy childhood would be an understatement! He would often proudly tell you of the glorious days growing up in the 1980s in 69 Bralsford Road. His school on Mauldeth Road, the music of the era (Joe thought Michael Jackson's 'Thriller' was the greatest phenomenon ever!) He loved classic television of of the 80s, classics such as the Knight Rider and the A-Team and of course, Joe had an impressive toy collection of this memorabilia courtesy of our parents! And of course is beloved Manchester United.

Talking about Joe's childhood, would not be complete without mentioning a very person, who became the fourth child of the Tucker family, Lee, it seemed was always in our house and the two struck a friendship that lasted the distance and test of time for over twenty years. That was one of the amazing characteristics about Joe. His loyalty was unshakeable. He felt strongly about friendship and trust.

Joe sailed pretty much sailed through childhood to adolescence with ease. Joe was always a good boy, never gave mum and dad any trouble! Always a joker and was very good at fixing things around the house from a young age. Secondary school, college and then university followed, while keeping down a part time and eventually full time job at Sainsbury's. He met some great friends here and would always bring home treats for us! Thankfully, Joe got to travel to see his friends and family in Grenada, Sierra Leone, New York and Germany. To Joe no other place really mattered in the world, these places were where we had family and that's all that mattered.

We could not ask for better brother than Joe. He was a wonderful role model to us and it's going to be a major life adjustment without our Joe. We were like the three musketeers! Joe was our best friend, music, museum cinema, eating out and gym companion. He was also our DIY and IT man, (very often we would call Joe and he would give us instructions over the phone) gossip buddy and he loved to provide television commentary via telephone and we very often had three or sometimes four way conversations as to what is on TV.

Most importantly, Joe took a huge amount of interest in our lives and our friends. He was very protective, encouraging and always wanted the very best for us. Sometimes we felt like Joe's big sisters too. He would ask for our advice on everything whether it was moral dilemmas, fashion advice, how he should decorate his flat, what I shouldl buy for dinner! He really valued our opinions. Jasmine (I) will tell you fondly that and proudly that she taught Joe how to tie his shoe laces, or the time when they were play fighting in the Abbey National Bank one day, and Joe accidentally punched out Jasmine's tooth. Or the time when we were in Grenada exploring, and Joe told me to step on a rock, which he knew was slippery and I flew into the air and landed on my back.

We will miss Joe's constant chatter, a trait which used to get him into trouble at school, his legendary appetite for food and his singing. When there was a moment of silence, you knew Joe had dozed off to sleep!

His hospitality was adorable! If any one had the great pleasure of going to Joe's house, he would love to make a fuss over you! He loved company. He would make sure you were well watered and fed, entertained, comfortable and happy. If you were happy, then Joe was happy.

After landing his position at the Inland Revenue, Joe worked there for about five years or so before being transferred to Manchester. We were happy and excited for him, just as he was, as we knew he would be going to live back "home".

And he was. He enjoyed living in his flat. Everything he needed was in close proximity, just as he liked it. His workplace, friends, family, shopping, entertainment and the added bonus that he was not too far from the Old Trafford football ground. That was another thing about Joe. He was a really simple and uncomplicated man. He did not like fuss, arguments or any tension surrounding him whatsoever. Despite the distance, we were only a telephone call away and Joe would always come down to London to spend a weekend with us. Who knew that his visit on Thursday, 5th February 2009, would be his last?

Joe was a beloved nephew, cousin, friend, colleague but the role of being a wonderful brother and son, meant more to him than anything. Joe loved and respected his parents deeply and he made our parents extremely proud. Joe was Dad's football and driving companion. Joe would go to Dad's events that we did not want go to sometimes. When Joe came down forhis visits from Manchester, he would still go shopping with Dad. And Joe would have no shame and would proudly tell you he was a mamma's boy! He loved his mother so much in every possible way. The older we got, the more we became more like friends with our parents. It was the Tucker family tradition to go out for a meal to celebrate a birthday, jokes and laughter were always a plenty when the five of us where together.

Memories like this we will treasure for ever. Our beloved Joe, you left us too soon and too suddenly and darling we miss you desperately. We still feel you, man. To our Son, Brother, Best Friend and Angel, your sprit will remain with us eternally.

Love always, The Tuckers

From: Bill

I stand before you today to pay tribute to Joe, on behalf of all his friends and colleagues who worked alongside him at Her Majesty's Revenue and Customs.

In short, Joe was the sort of person we all wanted to work with. He was thoughtful, polite and had tremendous enthusiasm not just for his job but for life in general. He clearly loved his family and spoke of his Mum and Dad in particular on many occasions whilst he was at work.

It is a tragedy beyond words that we have lost Joe at such a young age.

Over the last few weeks we have all had many conversations about Joe and what he has meant to each of us personally. We in HMRC wanted this tribute to be a reflection of everyone's memories of Joe and many of his colleagues have contributed their own thoughts and recollections.

We always knew that the most important part of Joe's life was his family. When he went on a business trip to Edinburgh recently, he insisted on searching around Princess Street to find his Mum some genuine Scottish shortbread. His manager Sandra remembers how enthralled and excited he was by Edinburgh. Joe commented that it was just like Paris – but he thought it did need a river just by the station to be really similar! We don't know if Joe had ever been to Paris, but it didn't matter because we knew what Joe meant. His excitement at doing and seeing things for the first time was quite infectious and really endearing.

We were always impressed by how smartly dressed Joe was – except when he cycled to work in his trainers. Jackie, his manager at the time, once asked him why he only changed into his highly polished shoes in the office as he was so particular about his appearance. Joe explained that this was because of his Dad's advice – he once advised Joe to always ensure his shoes were shiny as this would impress people!

When he went with one of his work colleagues Matt to Old Trafford for the first time since Joe came back to Manchester, Joe was taking lots of photographs of the players and the ground and was so excited at watching Manchester United beat Portsmouth. Joe's favourite player was Ryan Giggs and some in the office tried to persuade him that it should be Eric Cantona – but Joe insisted that Ryan Giggs was the best.

In preparing this tribute, I realised that it is so difficult to get across to everyone here today all the lovely comments and memories that we have received about Joe in the last few weeks. I think that the best I can do is to let those comments speak for themselves. The following represents a small selection of the comments I have received about Joe:

Joe was very family orientated – he really loved and respected his Mum and Dad;

He was such a lovely humble person;

Joe was always prepared to finish off any cakes that were left in the office – he loved the chocolate fudge cakes!;

He really loved his job and was wonderful to work with;

I never once heard him complain or moan about anything – he always seemed happy.

He was Mr Cool – we were all jealous of his good looks, natural charm and thoughtfulness.

From a personal point of view, I will miss Joe very much. I will miss his gentle humour, the chats we used to have about football – I am a Manchester City supporter – and I will miss someone who was an excellent Officer and role model for HM Revenue and Customs.

Finally, I would like to also pay tribute to Joe's parents, Sigismund and Joan. I first met them in the immediate aftermath following Joe's death when they came up to Manchester to meet some of his colleagues and see where he worked. Although I had never met them or spoken with them before, I knew that they would be loving and caring *people – you cannot bring up someone of the quality of Joe without having these attributes yourself.*

I would also like to say that Sigismund and Joan have carried themselves with enormous dignity through what is an unimaginably dreadful period for both them and all of Joe's family. All I can say is that they can be proud of their son Joe, proud of how much affection everyone who met Joe had for him and proud of a son who loved his family more than anything else.

We in Revenue and Customs are all still shocked and stunned at losing Joe. But as these painful feelings fade and give way to happy memories, I am certain that we will always remember Joe's smile that lit up the room, his natural enthusiasm for life, his charm and thoughtfulness towards others and the joy he got from being with his family.

We will miss you Joe, but we will never forget you.

From: Lesley Strathie, Chief Executive, HM Revenue & Customs

As Chief Executive of HM Revenue & Customs, I wanted to write to you both to say how very sorry I was to learn of the recent death of your son Joe.

This must be a very difficult and emotional time for you and your family and I would like you to know that the thoughts of Joe's friends and colleagues in the department are very much with you all at this sad time. I hope that it will be some comfort to you to know how highly Joe was regarded, both professionally and personally, by everyone who worked with him in HMRC. He will be sadly missed. I send my deepest sympathy to you both.

From: Angela Day

I write to you today in deep sorrow, sharing with you in your great loss. I had the privilege of knowing Joe simply to chat about the day's events and to share a few cheery words each day in the Revenue and Customs office on the fourth floor, Ralie Quays. He unfailingly lifted my spirit with his lovely smile, his courtesy and his helpfulness. He was a wonderful colleague who made the office a nicer place: Joe had that gift in abundance. I can't imagine what you must be going through at this time. My hope and my prayer is that you will find some comfort through knowing how much he was valued and loved by his colleagues who will never forget him. My thoughts, my heart, and my love go out to you all. Take care of each other, and be at peace. God bless always.

From: Anne Suthers, Business Improvement, Corporate & Change Team, B&C Delivery

I've only just heard the awful news about Joe. Feel completely in shock myself, so can't possibly imagine how devastated you must all be feeling. Just to let you all know that I am thinking of you all and sending lots of hugs.

From: Julie Fletcher, Local Lean Expert, NOS Wolverhampton

Just a quick email to say I was really sorry to hear about Joe. I saw the intranet message yesterday as I had been out of the office on Tuesday. I didn't know him that well but he always stayed in my mind for how positive he was regarding the Pacesetter tools (especially Paretos!). I don't come across many people like him in my role and I'm sure the teams up there will definitely miss him. Please pass on my condolences to your guys.

From: David Berry (KAI Information Services)

I've just learned the sad news about Joe. I didn't really know him or even know his name, but we'd always exchange a few words about United. My sympathies go to you and the team and naturally to his family.

From: Sandra Wells, (CustOPS)

I can not really put into words how truly sorry I am about the death of Joseph. I know that to lose the young man you loved so much must seem too hard to bear, and no words can truly comfort the mixed emotions that must be going on inside. Please please be glad for all the special times you had and although at the moment you will find it hard Joseph's memory will always be beside you and never fade away. Take care, my love and thoughts are with you all.

From: Sharon O'Neill, Management Support Team Leader Solicitors Office, HM Revenue & Customs

I was very sad to hear the news this afternoon regarding the death of Joe. Many of my colleagues in the Solicitors office knew Joe and are also very deeply saddened by the news. I have spoken with Tracey Buckley this afternoon and I have passed on our thoughts to you and your team and also to Joe's family. I am sure there is nothing we can do to ease your team's sadness but if there is anything you need please let me know.

From: Chris Jones (National Clearance Hub)

I have just heard the very sad news about Joe. Please pass on my thoughts to his family and to the staff in the central team as this must have come as a great shock. It goes without saying that if there is anything I can do please do not hesitate to call.

Dear Mr & Mrs Tucker

Firstly may we introduce ourselves; our names are John Faulds and Tracy Heam, we were Joseph's neighbours and known him since he moved onto Regents Park. We were devastated to hear that Joseph passed away. We just would like to say he was friendly, down to earth guy, a true gentleman. In all honestly, he was the best neighbour we have ever had and will be sadly missed.

We cannot imagine the grief and pain you and your family is going through. Our thoughts and prayers are with you during this difficult time.

Yours Faithfully,

John and Tracy

From Joe's workmates:

J.J,

A true gent and a pleasure to work with. They say only the good die young and it's certainly true in your case. May your soul rest in peace. God Bless,
Dee

A great guy who was greatly missed since he moved away and someone who will never be forgotten now he has left us all. God bless Joseph,
Peter

I worked closely with Joe for three years and always found him to be a friendly and easy going guy. He had an innate knack for getting on with everyone and was highly popular (despite his proud support for Manchester United!)

He was a great guy who will be sorely missed by all. My heartfelt condolences go out to his nearest and dearest.
Alan

It has been a great pleasure to have known Joseph, a great man with a big heart, full of respect for all around him, full of happiness and most of all full of life. We have been blessed to know you. May your soul rest in peace.
Nalini

It was a real pleasure to know Joseph. Always the friendly smiling guy. Joseph will be greatly missed and I will certainly miss our football banter. I'm sure Joseph is in a better place now.
God Bless,
Dave N

Joe,
You were loved and sorely missed by all that knew you. You were kind, courteous and a true gentleman. You untimely departure left us all in shock. May almighty God rest your gentle soul in peace.
Kay

Joseph was my manager at New Kings Beam House. He was kind, polite, hardworking and respectful. I remember thinking on more than one occasion, your parents must be so proud of you, Joseph. You are a credit to them and indeed he was. I am so saddened at this loss and I pray that Joseph rests in peace with the Lord.
God Bless Joseph,
Julia

Till we meet again dear friend. God be with you. Joseph was a pleasant person to be around and always treated everyone well. He was always ready to listen and help out in any way he could.

As my manager, I remember in my time of trouble he encouraged and helped me get back to work when I almost left due to personal problems.

Indeed he was a great man, friend and brother and I always thank God for his life.

Rest in perfect peace,
Kofi

To my mate Joseph,
You were my manager, but I was lucky enough to call you

friend. I'll miss the laughs we had and the good times we shared both in and out of the office. You were well regarded by one and all and your unexpected departure has shocked and saddened me deeply.

It seems the almighty had other plans for you Joe, so may you rest in peace knowing that those you've left behind will forever hold you in their fondest memories.
Riz

═══════════════════════════════

Joseph was my manager, although I worked from Crown Building, he was such a kind, polite, helpful and respectful person. It was such a shock and I am so saddened by this loss and pray that Joseph's soul rests in peace with the lord Jesus Christ.
God Bless Joseph,
Jay

═══════════════════════════════

Joseph dear,
I never knew Saturday 29th November 2008 would be the last time. When we met at the collegiate ex pupil dance at Holborn. You asked me to dance with you whilst you told me how much you're enjoying your work in Manchester. Always cheerful, respectful and intelligent too. May you rest in perfect peace in the safe arms of our Lord Jesus Christ.

To the parents and the rest of the family, no words or sympathy could erase the pain and loss of your beloved Joseph. But may the memories bring comfort in your sorrow and peace in your hearts.
Combra una oush fao una pikin.
God Bless you all,
Vicky Hume

Joseph was a respectful, well brought up guy, a joy to any parent. I told he would make a good husband to someone, someday not knowing it would never happen. He was hardworking and good team player, he got along with everyone in the office, always had a smile on his face. Whenever I worked from the Waterloo office, we all went out together for lunch, we had a few laughs at Christmas meals. He was not a member of my team, but he was always at our meals. Even after moving to Manchester, he still attended the next meal. When we told him that would be the last Christmas meal as a team, as the project was coming to an end, I never knew that would be the last time I would see him alive.

Joseph your death has come as a great shock but I know you are in a better place.
Rest in perfect peace,
Bola

Joseph,
I never dreamt that when we met up in Manchester last year that I would never see you again. You were a good friend, kind, considerate, helpful and always there to listen.

They say God takes the best first and that is so true. Rest in peace Joe, you will never be forgotten. It was a privilege to know you.
Barbara

Joseph,
You will be missed. You were a true gent and a good friend. Rest in peace.
Victoria

Everyone who came in contact with him liked Joseph. The thing that I respected about him the most was that he never spoke badly of anyone. He was always kind, patient and loving. He is a loss to this world. May he rest in peace.
Cordelia

Joseph,
In the few years I have known and worked with you, it was a great pleasure. You were really hard working and a good friend to all your work colleagues. Never bad word to say about anyone. Always kind and gentle. It was a privilege to know you. I am so sad that your gone, but ask that God show you favour as you rest in peace.
Linda

Joseph Tucker
You were my manager. I came from Hithrow. So close we were. I learned much from you. You showed me around. You left us to go somewhere, now we've lost you forever. You were great. May your soul rest in perfect peace.
Your friend,
Chris Asangana

Joe,
I'm never one with words, but could fill the rest of this book in explaining what a great guy you 'Are'. I'm sure your family already knows this.

I'm gutted you wont be joining me for the Sunderland - Man United game but will save you a seat in case you feel like popping down.

You were a great manager but an even better friend. I hope during days your mum and dad feel low, they hold on to the great thoughts and memories you leave. Never forgotten, mate. You were one of the true best.
Andrew

It was a great pleasure to have known such a lovely, caring and friendly man. He was a very well respected person. He will be missed by all that knew him. God bless you, one day we will meet again,
Sheila

A great guy and a real pleasure to work with. He will be missed. Personally I'll miss his emails every couple of months.
Joho

Printed in the United States
By Bookmasters

THE TALE
OF
TIMMY TIPTOES

ONCE upon a time there was a little fat comfortable grey squirrel, called Timmy Tiptoes. He had a nest thatched with leaves in the top of a tall tree ; and he had a little squirrel wife called Goody.

TIMMY TIPTOES sat out,
enjoying the breeze; he
whisked his tail and chuckled
—" Little wife Goody, the nuts
are ripe; we must lay up a
store for winter and spring."
Goody Tiptoes was busy
pushing moss under the
thatch—" The nest is so
snug, we shall be sound asleep
all winter." " Then we shall
wake up all the thinner, when
there is nothing to eat in
spring-time," replied prudent
Timothy.

THE TALE OF
TIMMY TIPTOES

By

BEATRIX POTTER

Author of
"The Tale of Peter Rabbit" etc.

FREDERICK WARNE

*The reproductions in this book have been made using
the most modern electronic scanning methods from entirely
new transparencies of Beatrix Potter's original watercolours.
They enable Beatrix Potter's skill as an artist to be appreciated
as never before, not even during her own lifetime.*

FREDERICK WARNE

Penguin Books Ltd, 27 Wrights Lane, London w8 5tz (Publishing and Editorial)
and Harmondsworth, Middlesex, England (Distribution and Warehouse)
Viking Penguin Inc., 40 West 23rd Street, New York, New York 10010, U.S.A.
Penguin Books Australia Ltd, Ringwood, Victoria, Australia
Penguin Books Canada Limited, 2801 John Street, Markham, Ontario, Canada l3r 1b4
Penguin Books (N.Z.) Ltd, 182–190 Wairau Road, Auckland 10, New Zealand

First published 1911
This edition with new reproductions first published 1987
This impression 1987

Colour reproduction by
East Anglian Engraving Company Ltd, Norwich
Printed and bound in Great Britain by
William Clowes Limited, Beccles and London

0388

FOR
MANY UNKNOWN LITTLE FRIENDS,
INCLUDING MONICA

WHEN Timmy and Goody
Tiptoes came to the
nut thicket, they found other
squirrels were there already.

Timmy took off his jacket
and hung it on a twig ; they
worked away quietly by themselves.

EVERY day they made several journeys and picked quantities of nuts. They carried them away in bags, and stored them in several hollow stumps near the tree where they had built their nest.

WHEN these stumps were full, they began to empty the bags into a hole high up a tree, that had belonged to a wood-pecker; the nuts rattled down — down — down inside.

"How shall you ever get them out again? It is like a money-box!" said Goody.

"I shall be much thinner before spring-time, my love," said Timmy Tiptoes, peeping into the hole.

THEY did collect quantities
—because they did not
lose them ! Squirrels who bury
their nuts in the ground lose
more than half, because they
cannot remember the place.

The most forgetful squirrel
in the wood was called Silvertail. He began to dig, and
he could not remember. And
then he dug again and found
some nuts that did not belong
to him ; and there was a fight.
And other squirrels began to
dig,—the whole wood was in
commotion !

UNFORTUNATELY, just at this time a flock of little birds flew by, from bush to bush, searching for green caterpillars and spiders. There were several sorts of little birds, twittering different songs.

The first one sang— "Who's bin digging-up *my* nuts ? Who's-been-digging-up *my* nuts ? "

And another sang—" Little bita bread and - *no* - cheese ! Little bit - a - bread an' - *no* - cheese ! "

THE squirrels followed and listened. The first little bird flew into the bush where Timmy and Goody Tiptoes were quietly tying up their bags, and it sang—" Who's-bin digging-up *my* nuts ? Who's been digging-up *my*-nuts ? "

Timmy Tiptoes went on with his work without re-plying ; indeed, the little bird did not expect an answer. It was only singing its natural song, and it meant nothing at all.

BUT when the other squirrels heard that song, they rushed upon Timmy Tiptoes and cuffed and scratched him, and upset his bag of nuts. The innocent little bird which had caused all the mischief, flew away in a fright!

Timmy rolled over and over, and then turned tail and fled towards his nest, followed by a crowd of squirrels shouting —" Who's - been digging - up *my*-nuts ? "

THEY caught him and dragged him up the very same tree, where there was the little round hole, and they pushed him in. The hole was much too small for Timmy Tiptoes' figure. They squeezed him dreadfully, it was a wonder they did not break his ribs. " We will leave him here till he confesses," said Silvertail Squirrel, and he shouted into the hole—

" Who's - been - digging - up *my*-nuts ? "

TIMMY TIPTOES made
no reply ; he had tumbled
down inside the tree, upon
half a peck of nuts belonging
to himself. He lay quite
stunned and still.

GOODY TIPTOES picked up the nut bags and went home. She made a cup of tea for Timmy ; but he didn't come and didn't come.

Goody Tiptoes passed a lonely and unhappy night. Next morning she ventured back to the nut-bushes to look for him ; but the other unkind squirrels drove her away.

She wandered all over the wood, calling—

" Timmy Tiptoes ! Timmy Tiptoes ! Oh, where is Timmy Tiptoes ? "

IN the meantime Timmy Tiptoes came to his senses. He found himself tucked up in a little moss bed, very much in the dark, feeling sore ; it seemed to be under ground. Timmy coughed and groaned, because his ribs hurted him. There was a chirpy noise, and a small striped Chipmunk appeared with a night light, and hoped he felt better ?

It was most kind to Timmy Tiptoes ; it lent him its night-cap ; and the house was full of provisions.

THE Chipmunk explained that it had rained nuts through the top of the tree —" Besides, I found a few buried ! " It laughed and chuckled when it heard Timmy's story. While Timmy was confined to bed, it 'ticed him to eat quantities—" But how shall I ever get out through that hole unless I thin myself ? My wife will be anxious ! " " Just another nut —or two nuts ; let me crack them for you," said the Chipmunk. Timmy Tiptoes grew fatter and fatter !

NOW Goody Tiptoes had set to work again by herself. She did not put any more nuts into the wood-pecker's hole, because she had always doubted how they could be got out again. She hid them under a tree root; they rattled down, down, down. Once when Goody emptied an extra big bagful, there was a decided squeak; and next time Goody brought another bagful, a little striped Chipmunk scrambled out in a hurry.

"IT is getting perfectly full-up down-stairs; the sitting-room is full, and they are rolling along the passage; and my husband, Chippy Hackee, has run away and left me. What is the explanation of these showers of nuts?"

"I am sure I beg your pardon; I did not not know that anybody lived here," said Mrs. Goody Tiptoes; "but where is Chippy Hackee? My husband, Timmy Tiptoes, has run away too." "I know where Chippy is; a little bird told me," said Mrs. Chippy Hackee.

SHE led the way to the woodpecker's tree, and they listened at the hole.

Down below there was a noise of nut crackers, and a fat squirrel voice and a thin squirrel voice were singing together—

" My little old man and I fell out,
How shall we bring this matter about ?
Bring it about as well as you can,
And get you gone, you little old man ! "

" YOU could squeeze in, through that little round hole," said Goody Tiptoes. " Yes, I could," said the Chipmunk, " but my husband, Chippy Hackee, bites ! "

Down below there was a noise of cracking nuts and nibbling ; and then the fat squirrel voice and the thin squirrel voice sang—

" For the diddlum day
    Day diddle dum di !
    Day diddle diddle dum day ! "

BUT Chippy Hackee con-
tinued to camp out for
another week, although it was
uncomfortable.

AT last a large bear came walking through the wood. Perhaps he also was looking for nuts ; he seemed to be sniffing around.

CHIPPY HACKEE went home in a hurry !

AND when Chippy Hackee got home, he found he had caught a cold in his head ; and he was more uncomfortable still.

A^{nd} now Timmy and Goody Tiptoes keep their nut-store fastened up with a little padlock.

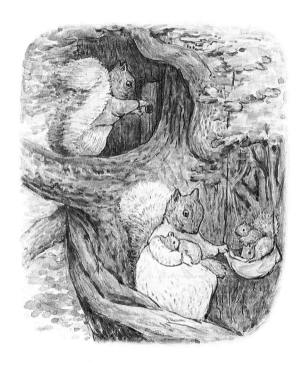

AND whenever that little bird sees the Chipmunks, he sings — " Who's - been - digging-up *my*-nuts ?   Who's been digging-up *my*-nuts ? " But nobody ever answers !

THE END